The New Seattle Cookbook

Discover Delicious West Coast Meals from the Heart of Seattle

By
BookSumo Press
All rights reserved

Published:
http://www.booksumo.com

LEGAL NOTES

All Rights Reserved. No Part Of This Book May Be Reproduced Or Transmitted In Any Form Or By Any Means. Photocopying, Posting Online, And / Or Digital Copying Is Strictly Prohibited Unless Written Permission Is Granted By The Book's Publishing Company. Limited Use Of The Book's Text Is Permitted For Use In Reviews Written For The Public.

Table of Contents

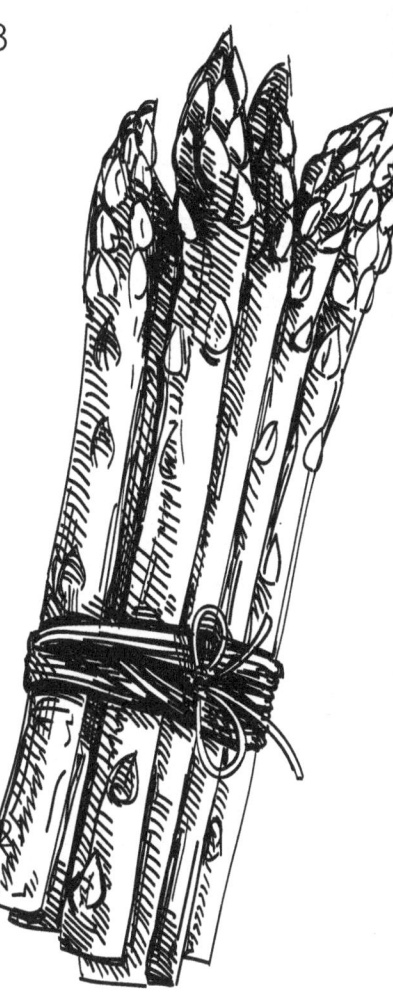

Seattle Quinoa Bowls 7

Seattle Fruit Salad with Citrus Glaze 8

Seattle White Bean Soup 9

2-Ingredient Pie Filling 10

Full Quinoa Salad from Seattle 11

Puget Park Street Dogs 12

How to Make a Pie Crust 13

Authentic Seafood Chowder 14

Cornbread Washington Style 15

Angela's Frost Cake 16

Squash Stew 17

Seattle Lentil Hot Pot 18

Washington State Fair Popcorn 19

Mango & Raisin Chutney 20

Chicken Curry with Mango Chutney

Kiara's Blueberry Pie 22

Crepes Ballard 23

Kiara's Blueberry Pie 24

Spinach Salad with Poppy Seed Vinaigrette 25

Lake City Lasagna 26

Seattle Café Tofu Spring Rolls 27

Artisanal Broccoli Dinner 28

Pine Chicken Rolls 29

Artisanal French Onion Soup 30

Rachel's Rasp Pie 31
Pacific Ocean Pie 32
Country Cobbler With Streusel 34
Asian Style Soba Salad 35
Hillman Café Potato Soup 36
Feta Artichoke Salad 37
New Holly Pilaf 38
Onion Soup Stroganoff 39
Citrus Chicken Thighs with Seattle Cream Glaze 40
Simple Torta 41
Seattle Mushroom Gratin 42
Cheesy Glazed Asparagus 43
Scalloped Potatoes in Seattle 44
Shortbread Cookies 45
Roxy's Apple Bites 46
Martha Washington Pops 47
Vietnamese Pho I (Rice Noodle Soup) 48
Full Macaroni Salad in Seattle 49
Cherry Caprese Kabobs with Lemon Dressing 50
Alaskan Salmon Dip 51
Alternative Blackberry Crisp (Slump) 52
Seattle Late-September Muffins 53
Hot Smokie Crescents 54
Pear Tart with Sugar Crumble Pie 55
Velveeta Tex Noodles 56
Sun Dried Pesto Sauce 57

Charred Bass with Jalapeno Salsa 58
Gonzaga Dorm Cookies 59
Rainier Vista Rollatini 60
Rice Pudding with Cherry Sauce 61
How to Smoke a Turkey 62
Mixed Green Salad with Berry Dressing 63
Authentic Beef and Broccoli 64
Seattle Spice Rub 65
Mushroom Sauce Meatballs 66
Bonnie's Black Beans 67
Seattle Couscous Salad 68
Romano Zucchini Boats 69
Seattle BBQ Sauce for Caterers 70
Wedding Soup 101 71
Apple Aoli 72
Chocolate Cake Brownies 73
Lemony Chicken Cutlets 74
Seattle Coffee Stew 75
Hot Dogs Seattle Style 76
Seattle Tapenade 77
Artisanal Chicken Salad 78
Tarragon Zucchini 79
Washington Country Turkey Roast 80
Beacon Hill Brussels Sprouts 81
Seattle Compote 82
Baguette Lunch Box Salad 83

Chicken Soup Seattle 84

Seattle Red Potato Salad 85

Simple Cream of Meatball 86

Leschi Park Avocado Shrimp Croissants 87

Lox Beau Monde Sandwiches 88

Butterscotch Squares from Seattle 89

Sweet Ginger Cookies 90

Tomatoes Stuffed 91

Mediterranean Seasoned Chicken with Yogurt Salsa 92

Enchiladas Washington Style 93

Isamelle's Enchiladas 94

Whipped Chocolate Pie 95

Madrona Chocolate Puffs 96

Spicy Tofu Pesto 97

Lake Washington Cookies 98

Perfect Seattle Chili 99

Jalapeno Maple Chili 100

Seattle Quinoa Bowls

Prep Time: 10 mins
Total Time: 25 mins

Servings per Recipe: 6
Calories   210.2
Fat   11.8g
Cholesterol   0.0mg
Sodium   58.1mg
Carbohydrates   22.6g
Protein   5.1g

Ingredients

Vinaigrette
2 tbsp extra virgin olive oil
2 tbsp lemon juice
2 tbsp seasoned rice vinegar
1 garlic clove, minced
sea salt & ground black pepper
Salad
1 C. quinoa, rinsed and drained
2 C. water
2 C. chopped spinach
1 C. roasted chicken, shredded
1 medium avocado, peeled and chopped
1/4 C. sliced green onion
1/4 C. basil, chopped
8 kalamata olives, pitted and quartered
Optional Garnishes
steamed green beans
hard boiled eggs, sliced in half, or diced

Directions

1. For the vinaigrette: in a bowl, add all the ingredients and beat until well combined.
2. In a pan of the boiling water, cook the quinoa for about 15 minutes.
3. Remove from the heat and stir in vinaigrette and remaining ingredients and optional garnishes.
4. Enjoy.

SEATTLE
Fruit Salad with Citrus Glaze

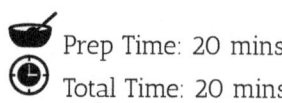

Prep Time: 20 mins
Total Time: 20 mins

Servings per Recipe: 15
Calories 131.9
Fat 0.6g
Cholesterol 0.0mg
Sodium 8.4mg
Carbohydrates 33.3g
Protein 1.8g

Ingredients
Salad
1 whole pineapple, peeled and diced
1 whole cantaloupe, peeled and diced
1 lb. strawberries, hulled and quartered
4 -5 nectarines, segmented
1/2 pint blackberries
1/2 pint blueberries
6 whole kiwi fruits, diced
Dressing
1/2 C. honey

1 large lime, juice and zest
1 - 2 tbsp grated ginger
1 - 2 tsp poppy seed

Directions
1. Get a small mixing bowl: Whisk in it the lime juice with ginger and poppy seed to make the dressing.
2. Get a serving bowl. Toss in it all the salad ingredients. Drizzle the dressing on top and top them to coat.
3. Place the salad in the fridge for few minutes then serve it.
4. Enjoy.

Seattle White Bean Soup

🍲 Prep Time: 20 mins
⏲ Total Time: 55 mins

Servings per Recipe: 6
Calories   330.1
Fat   17.3g
Cholesterol   21.5mg
Sodium   968.6mg
Carbohydrates   27.5g
Protein   19.1g

Ingredients

- 1/2 lb. mild Italian sausage, ground
- 2 tbsp olive oil
- 1/2 medium yellow onion, diced
- 1 medium carrot, diced
- 1 celery rib, diced
- 5 large garlic cloves, minced
- 1/8 tsp crushed red pepper flakes
- 1/2 tsp kosher salt
- 1/4 tsp ground black pepper
- 48 oz. organic low sodium chicken broth
- 2 C. cannellini beans
- 1 lb. kale, rinsed, stems removed, leaves torn into pieces
- 1 tbsp lemon juice
- 1/2 tsp grated lemon zest

Directions

1. Place a pot over medium heat. Heat in it 1 tbsp of olive oil. Cook in it the sausage for min.
2. Drain the crumbled sausage and place it aside.
3. Stir the remaining olive oil into the pot. Cook in it the onion for 3 min. Stir in the celery with carrot. Cook them for 3 min.
4. Add the garlic, pepper flakes, salt and black pepper. Cook them for 2 min. Stir in the chicken broth.
5. Let them cook over high heat until they start boiling. Lower the heat and stir in the cooked sausage with half of the cannellini beans.
6. Get a mixing bowl: Mash in it the remaining cannellini beans with a fork slightly. Add it to the soup.
7. Add the kale and let them soup cook for 16 to 22 min over low heat.
8. Adjust the seasoning of the soup then serve it hot.
9. Enjoy.

2-INGREDIENT
Pie Filling

🥣 Prep Time: 7 mins
🕐 Total Time: 7 mins

Servings per Recipe: 8
Calories   252.0
Fat   22.0g
Cholesterol   81.5mg
Sodium   201.3mg
Carbohydrates   13.1g
Protein   1.2g

Ingredients
1 pint heavy whipping cream
1 (3 1/2 ounce) boxes instant pudding mix

Directions
1. Get a mixing bowl. Let cool down in the fridge for at least 10 min.
2. Pour the whipping cream into the mixing bowl. Beat it until it starts to become thick.
3. Add the pudding mi gradually while beating them until they become thick.
4. Spoon the cream into a pie crust.
5. Garnish it with your favorite toppings and chill it in the fridge for at least 1 h.
6. Enjoy.

Full Quinoa Salad from Seattle

Prep Time: 15 mins
Total Time: 30 mins

Servings per Recipe: 4
Calories	510.3
Fat	22.1g
Cholesterol	0.0mg
Sodium	995.2mg
Carbohydrates	67.5g
Protein	15.8g

Ingredients

- 3/4 C. quinoa, rinsed and drained
- 1 1/2 C. water
- 1 tsp garlic, minced
- 2 tbsp extra virgin olive oil
- 1/4 C. lemon juice
- 2 tsp grated lemon zest
- 1/2 C. cucumber, peeled, seeded & diced
- 1 (15 ounce) cans garbanzo beans, drained
- 1 tbsp dill, chopped
- 1/2 C. parsley, chopped
- 1/2 C. golden raisin
- 2/3 C. almonds, toasted & chopped
- 1/4 C. green onion, sliced
- 1/4 C. carrot, grated
- 1 tsp sea salt
- 1/4 tsp ground black pepper

Directions

1. Place a saucepan over medium heat. Place in it the quinoa and cover it with water.
2. Let it cook until it starts boiling. Lower the heat and put on the lid. Let it cook for 16 min until the quinoa is done.
3. Once the time is up, turn off the heat and let the quinoa sit covered for 12 min.
4. Remove the cover and stir it with a fork.
5. Get a mixing bowl: Toss in it the quinoa with the remaining ingredients. Mix them well.
6. Adjust the seasoning of your salad then serve it right away.
7. Enjoy.

PUGET PARK
Street Dogs

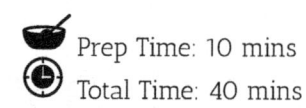

🥣 Prep Time: 10 mins
🕐 Total Time: 40 mins

Servings per Recipe: 2
Calories   477.2
Fat   33.9g
Cholesterol   75.7mg
Sodium   874.9mg
Carbohydrates   31.0g
Protein   12.3g

Ingredients
2 hot dogs
2 hot dog buns
1 onion, halved and sliced
1 tsp oil
1 tsp butter

1/2 tsp brown sugar
salt
pepper
3 oz. cream cheese

Directions
1. Place a pan over medium heat. Heat in it the butter until it melts. Caramelized in it the onion with sugar for 22 min over low heat.
2. Sprinkle some salt and pepper over the onion to season it.
3. Place a heavy saucepan over medium heat. Stir in it the cream cheese until it becomes warm and soft.
4. Prepare the hot dogs by following the instructions on the package. Butter the bread buns and toast them.
5. Spoon the soft cream cheese into the buns and spread it. Lay over them the hot dogs with the caramelized onion.
6. Serve your hot dogs right away with your favorite toppings.
7. Enjoy.

How to Make a Pie Crust

Prep Time: 15 mins
Total Time: 15 mins

Servings per Recipe: 8
Calories 360.6
Fat 24.3g
Cholesterol 63.4mg
Sodium 298.5mg
Carbohydrates 31.5g
Protein 4.3g

Ingredients

2 1/2 C. unbleached all-purpose flour
1 tsp table salt
1 tbsp granulated sugar
16 tbsp unsalted butter

3 tbsp sour cream
1/3 C. ice water

Directions

1. Get a small mixing bowl: Whisk in it the sour cream with ice water.
2. Slice the butter into dices. Place it in the freeze and let it sit for 11 min.
3. Get a food processor: Combine in it the flour with salt and sugar well.
4. Mix in the butter with sour cream and water mix gradually until they become smooth.
5. Shape the dough into two balls. Roll them into 4 inches circles. Cover each one of them with a piece of plastic wrap.
6. Place the dough balls aside for 1 h 1 h 30 min.
7. Once the time is up, flatten the dough into the shape and size of your pie pans.
8. Freeze your crust or use it right away with your favorite filling.
9. Enjoy.

AUTHENTIC
Seafood Chowder

Prep Time: 20 mins
Total Time: 50 mins

Servings per Recipe: 6
Calories 295.4
Fat 9.2g
Cholesterol 50.8mg
Sodium 203.5mg
Carbohydrates 30.9g
Protein 23.7g

Ingredients
1 lb. salmon fillet, skin and bones removed, rinsed and dried
1 tbsp cooking oil
2 C. chopped carrots
1 C. chopped onion
1/2 C. chopped red pepper
1/2 C. chopped celery
1 1/2 C. water
4 C. low sodium chicken broth
2 1/2 C. cubed red potatoes
1 C. corn kernel
2 C. milk
2 tbsp cornstarch
2 tsp dill
1 pinch salt

Directions
1. Place a saucepan over medium heat. Heat in it the oil. Sauté in it the carrots, onion, pepper, and celery for 11 min.
2. Place a large saucepan of over medium high heat. Heat it until it starts boiling.
3. Stir in the salmon and let them cook until it starts boiling again. Lower the heat and put on the lid. let them cook for 7 to 9 min.
4. Drain the salmon and place it aside to cool down for few minutes. Cut it into 1/2 inch pieces.
5. Place a pot over medium heat. Combine in it the broth, potatoes, corn, dill, and salt. Cook them until they start boiling.
6. Put on the lid and let them cook for 16 min over low heat.
7. Get a mixing bowl: Whisk in it the cornstarch with milk until no lumps are found. Stir it into the soup pot with the rest of the milk.
8. Let them cook over medium heat until the chowder starts boiling. Season the chowder with some salt and pepper.
9. Let it cook for an extra 2 to 3 min. Stir in the flaked salmon then serve your chowder hot.
10. Enjoy.

Cornbread Washington Style

Prep Time: 5 mins
Total Time: 40 mins

Servings per Recipe: 9
Calories   312.9
Fat   16.9g
Cholesterol   72.8mg
Sodium   409.4mg
Carbohydrates   35.6g
Protein   5.2g

Ingredients

- 2 C. Bisquick baking mix
- 1/2 C. cornmeal
- 1/2 C. sugar
- 1/2 C. real butter, melted
- 2 large eggs
- 1 C. milk

Directions

1. Before you do anything, preheat the oven to 350 F. Coat a bread pan with some butter.
2. Get a mixing bowl: Beat in it the eggs.
3. Mix in it the sugar, milk, with melted butter.
4. Stir in the cornmeal with bisquick until no lumps are found.
5. Pour the batter into the loaf pan. Place it in the oven and let it cook for 26 to 36 min.
6. Allow the bread to cool down in the pan until it cools down completely.
7. Serve it with your favorite toppings.
8. Enjoy.

ANGELA'S
Frost Cake

Prep Time: 40 mins
Total Time: 1 h 10 mins

Servings per Recipe: 16
Calories ≈ 750
Fat 596.2
Cholesterol 28.5g
Sodium 76.8mg
Carbohydrates 317.7mg
Protein 82.7g

Ingredients
Cake
2 1/2 C. all-purpose flour
1 3/4 C. sugar
1 1/2 tsp baking soda
1 tsp baking powder
1/2 tsp salt
1 C. vegetable oil
1 tbsp tangerine zest
1 C. tangerine juice
3 large eggs

1 C. sour cream
candied tangerine zest
Frosting
1 (8 ounce) packages cream cheese, softened
1/2 C. butter, softened
1 tbsp grated tangerine zest
3 tbsp tangerine juice
6 C. confectioners' sugar

Directions
1. Before you do anything, preheat the oven to 350 F.
2. To make the cake:
3. Before you do anything, preheat the oven to 350 F. Grease 2 baking pans with some cooking spray.
4. Get a mixing bowl: Mix in it the flour, sugar, baking soda, baking powder, and salt. Add the oil with zest, juice and eggs.
5. Beat them with an electric mixer until they become smooth.
6. Pour the batter into the greased pan. Place it in the oven and let it cook for 26 min.
7. To make the frosting:
8. Get a mixing bowl: Combine in it the cream cheese with butter with an electric mixer until they become light and smooth.
9. Add the tangerine juice and zest. Beat them until they become smooth.
10. Add the confectioner sugar gradually while beating them all the time.
11. Gently remove the cakes from the pan. Place them aside to cool down completely.
12. Cut the top of one cake to into an even layer. Spread over it some of the frosting.
13. Place over it the second cake. Coat broth cakes with the remaining frosting.
14. Garnish your cake with some tangerine segments and your other favorite toppings.
15. Enjoy.

Squash Stew

Prep Time: 10 mins
Total Time: 50 mins

Servings per Recipe: 4
Calories   388.2
Fat   27.1g
Cholesterol   78.9mg
Sodium   895.3mg
Carbohydrates   32.1g
Protein   8.4g

Ingredients

- 5 tbsp butter
- 1 large onion, diced
- 2 lbs. butternut squash, peeled, seeded and cut into pieces
- 4 C. chicken broth
- 1/2 tsp nutmeg
- 1/4 tsp cinnamon
- 1/2 C. whipping cream

Directions

1. Place a saucepan over medium heat. Heat in it the butter until it melts.
2. Cook in it the onion for 6 min. Stir in 4 C. of broth with cinnamon and nutmeg.
3. Add the squash and put on the lid. Let them cook for 22 min.
4. Get a food processor: Pour into it the soup and blend it smooth.
5. Pour the soup back into the saucepan with the whipping cream.
6. Heat the soup for few minutes then season it with some salt and pepper.
7. Serve your soup warm.
8. Enjoy.

SEATTLE
Lentil Hot Pot

Prep Time: 15 mins
Total Time: 1 h

Servings per Recipe: 6
Calories 262.7
Fat 5.4g
Cholesterol 10.9mg
Sodium 633.9mg
Carbohydrates 43.4g
Protein 12.3g

Ingredients

3/4 C. onion, chopped
3/4 C. celery, chopped
1 garlic clove, minced
2 tbsp butter
6 C. beef broth
1 (28 ounce) cans chopped tomatoes
3/4 C. dry lentils
3/4 C. pearl barley

1/2 tsp rosemary, crushed
1/2 tsp oregano, crushed
1/4 tsp pepper
1 C. carrot, sliced
1 C. Swiss cheese, shredded

Directions

1. Before you do anything, preheat the oven to 350 F.
2. To make the cake:
3. Before you do anything, preheat the oven to 350 F. Grease 2 baking pans with some cooking spray.
4. Get a mixing bowl: Mix in it the flour, sugar, baking soda, baking powder, and salt. Add the oil with zest, juice and eggs.
5. Beat them with an electric mixer until they become smooth.
6. Pour the batter into the greased pan. Place it in the oven and let it cook for 26 min.
7. To make the frosting:
8. Get a mixing bowl: Combine in it the cream cheese with butter with an electric mixer until they become light and smooth.
9. Add the tangerine juice and zest. Beat them until they become smooth.
10. Add the confectioner sugar gradually while beating them all the time.
11. Gently remove the cakes from the pan. Place them aside to cool down completely.
12. Cut the top of one cake to into an even layer. Spread over it some of the frosting.
13. Place over it the second cake. Coat broth cakes with the remaining frosting.
14. Garnish your cake with some tangerine segments and your other favorite toppings.
15. Enjoy.

Washington
State Fair Popcorn

🍲 Prep Time: 10 mins
🕒 Total Time: 25 mins

Servings per Recipe: 18
Calories   198.4
Fat   11.7g
Cholesterol   13.5mg
Sodium   152.5mg
Carbohydrates   21.4g
Protein   4.0g

Ingredients
18 C. popped popcorn
1 C. salted peanuts
1/2 C. butter

3/4 C. brown sugar
1/4 C. molasses

Directions
1. Before you do anything, preheat the oven to 350 F.
2. Follow the instructions on the package to prepare the popcorn.
3. Spread the popcorn on two lined up baking sheets. Drizzle over them the peanut butter.
4. Place a saucepan over medium heat. Stir in the butter until it melts. Add the molasses with brown sugar.
5. Heat them until they start boiling. Keep it boiling for 6 min to make the caramel sauce
6. Drizzle the sauce all over the popcorn.
7. Place the pans in the oven and let them cook for 16 min while stirring them every 3 to 4 min.
8. Serve your caramel corn.
9. Enjoy.

MANGO & RAISIN Chutney

Prep Time: 20 mins
Total Time: 1 h 5 mins

Servings per Recipe: 1
Calories 627.2
Fat 2.1g
Cholesterol 0.0mg
Sodium 3748.7mg
Carbohydrates 153.4g
Protein 4.2g

Ingredients
1 kg very firm mango
2 C. sugar
625 ml vinegar
1 (5 cm) pieces ginger, peeled
4 cloves garlic, peeled
2 - 4 tsps chili powder

4 tsps mustard seeds
8 tsps salt
1 C. raisins or 1 C. sultana

Directions
1. Peel the mango and then remove the pit and chop it.
2. In a pan, add sugar and vinegar, leaving about 20ml and simmer, stirring occasionally for about 10 minutes.
3. Meanwhile in a food processor, add remaining vinegar, garlic and ginger and pulse till a paste forms.
4. Transfer the paste into a pan and simmer, stirring continuously for about 10 minutes.
5. Stir in the mango and remaining ingredients and simmer, stirring occasionally for about 25 minutes or till desired thickness of chutney.
6. Transfer the chutney into hot sterilized jars and seal tightly and keep aside to cool.
7. This chutney can be stored in dark place for about 1 year but remember to refrigerate after opening.

Chicken Curry
with Mango Chutney

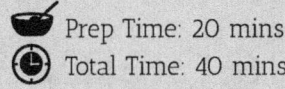 Prep Time: 20 mins
Total Time: 40 mins

Servings per Recipe: 6
Calories 535.4
Fat 34.1g
Cholesterol 226.8mg
Sodium 314.7mg
Carbohydrates 5.8g
Protein 50.1g

Ingredients

3 lbs. boneless skinless chicken breasts, sliced
1 medium onion, diced
2 1/2 tbsp vegetable oil
1/4 C. curry powder
1 C. mango chutney, pureed
1 1/2 C. whipping cream
1 pinch salt
green onion, chopped, tops only

Directions

1. Place a pan over medium heat. Heat in it the oil. Cook in it the onion for 4 min.
2. Stir in the curry powder and cook them for 3 min. Add the chutney with cream and a pinch of salt to make the sauce.
3. place a skillet over medium heat. Heat in it a splash of oil. Cook in it the chicken slices for 3 to 4 min on each side.
4. Stir in the chutney sauce. Let them cook for 12 min over low heat.
5. Serve your chicken chutney warm with some white rice.
6. Enjoy.

KIARA'S
Blueberry Pie

🥣 Prep Time: 30 mins
🕐 Total Time: 1 h

Servings per Recipe: 8
Calories	411.9
Fat	23.6g
Cholesterol	53.9mg
Sodium	194.7mg
Carbohydrates	48.2g
Protein	3.9g

Ingredients
1 9-inch pie shell, baked & cooled
6 oz. cream cheese, softened
1/2 C. confectioners' sugar
1/4 tsp vanilla extract
3/4 C. heavy whipping cream, whipped until stiff peaks are formed
2/3 C. granulated sugar
1/4 C. cornstarch

1/2 C. water
1/4 C. lemon juice
3 C. blueberries

Directions
1. Before you do anything, preheat the oven to 350 F.
2. Get a mixing bowl: Mix in it the soft cream cheese with vanilla and confectioner sugar until they become light and smooth.
3. Fold half of the whipped cream into the mixture. Add the remaining cream and fold it into the mix to make the filling.
4. Place a heavy saucepan over medium heat. Stir in the sugar, cornstarch, water and lemon juice.
5. Heat them until no lumps are found. Add the blueberries and let them cook for 3 min until the sauce becomes thick.
6. Turn off the heat and let the sauce cool down completely.
7. Spoon the cream filling into the pie crust and spread it in an even layer.
8. Drizzle over it the blueberries sauce. Place the tart in the fridge and let it for at least 60 min.
9. Serve your blueberry tart with your favorite toppings.
10. Enjoy.

Crepes Ballard

Prep Time: 10 mins
Total Time: 30 mins

Servings per Recipe: 3
Calories   405.0
Fat   8.4g
Cholesterol   141.0mg
Sodium   169.8mg
Carbohydrates   65.5g
Protein   15.2g

Ingredients
1 1/2 C. flour
1/2 tbsp sugar
1/2 tsp baking powder
1 1/2 C. milk
1/2 C. orange juice
2 eggs
1/2 tsp vanilla

1 tsp orange zest
1/2 C. orange juice
1 tsp cornstarch

Directions
1. Get a food processor: Combine in it the flour with sugar, baking powder, orange zest, cornstarch and salt.
2. Add the eggs gradually while mixing all the time followed by the milk, orange juice, and vanilla.
3. Keep them mixing until no lumps are found. Pour the batter into a mixing bowl and place it aside.
4. Place a large skillet over medium heat. Heat in it the oil.
5. Pour in it 1/4 C. of the batter. Swirl it in the pan into an even circle.
6. Cook the gallete until it set and become golden on the edges.
7. Flip it gently and cook it on the other side until it becomes golden.
8. Slid the galette into a plate. Repeat the process with the remaining batter.
9. Get a mixing bowl: Combine in it 1/2 C. of orange juice with 1 tsp of cornstarch until no lumps are found to make the sauce.
10. Place a small pan over medium heat. Pour in it the sauce and heat it until it becomes slightly thick.
11. Serve your orange sauce with the galettes then serve them with some fruit slices.
12. Enjoy.

ALASKAN
Grilled Salmon

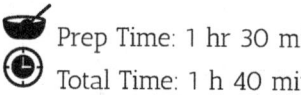 Prep Time: 1 hr 30 mins
Total Time: 1 h 40 mins

Servings per Recipe: 4
Calories 274.0
Fat 8.3g
Cholesterol 118.2mg
Sodium 327.3mg
Carbohydrates 1.2g
Protein 45.9g

Ingredients
2 -5 lbs. wild salmon fillets
1/4 C. prepared lemon mustard
1/4 tsp paprika
1/4 tsp cayenne pepper

Directions
1. Get a grilling plank. Soak it in water for at least 2 h before cooking. Drain it.
2. Before you do anything, preheat the grill.
3. Place the salmon fillets on the plank with the skin facing down.
4. Spread the mustard over the salmon fillet. Sprinkle over it the paprika followed by the cayenne pepper.
5. Place the salmon plank over the grill directly between the hot embers. Put on the grill lid and let it cook for 12 to 22 min until the salmon is done.
6. Once the time is up, remove the lid. Use a strong spatula with thongs to pull out the salmon plank.
7. Place it on aside and let it sit for at least 6 min. Transfer the salmon slices to a hot plates.
8. Serve your grilled salmon with a salad and your favorite toppings.
9. Enjoy.

Spinach Salad with Poppy Seed Vinaigrette

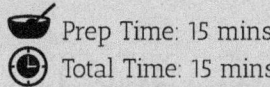

Prep Time: 15 mins
Total Time: 15 mins

Servings per Recipe: 10
Calories   249.3
Fat   19.0g
Cholesterol   0.0mg
Sodium   141.8mg
Carbohydrates   20.2g
Protein   2.0g

Ingredients

Salad
- 10 C. spinach
- 1/2 C. sliced red onion
- 1 pint strawberries, quartered*
- 1 (11 ounce) cans mandarin oranges, drained
- 1/2 C. chopped pecans, toasted

Vinaigrette
- 1/2 C. sugar
- 1/3 C. cider vinegar
- 2 tbsp lime juice
- 2 tbsp chopped red onions
- 1/2 tsp salt
- 2/3 C. vegetable oil
- 2 - 3 tsp poppy seeds

Directions

1. Get a blender: Place in it the sugar, vinegar, lime juice, onion and salt. Blend them smooth.
2. Add the oil gradually while blending them at the same time followed by the poppy seeds.
3. Get a serving bowl: Toss in it the red onion with strawberries, spinach and oranges. Drizzle some of the dressing on top.
4. Garnish the salad with the chopped pecans. Serve it with the remaining dressing.
5. Enjoy.

LAKE CITY
Lasagna

Prep Time: 45 mins
Total Time: 1 h 15 mins

Servings per Recipe: 6	
Calories	697.7
Fat	31.4g
Cholesterol	165.8mg
Sodium	1693.2mg
Carbohydrates	58.6g
Protein	44.9g

Ingredients

- 12 oz. lasagna noodles
- 2 tbsp salad oil
- 2 garlic cloves, minced
- 1 medium onion, chopped
- 1 lb. ground beef
- 1 1/2 tsp salt
- 1/4 tsp pepper
- 1/2 tsp rosemary
- 1 tbsp parsley, minced
- 12 oz. tomato paste
- 1 1/2 C. hot water
- 2 eggs, beaten
- 1 pint cottage cheese
- 1/2 lb. mozzarella cheese, sliced
- 1/4 C. parmesan cheese, grated

Directions

1. Before you do anything, preheat the oven to 350 F.
2. Prepare the lasagna pasta by following the instructions on the package. Drain it and place it aside.
3. Place a pan over medium heat. Heat in it the oil. Cook in it the onion with garlic for 3 min.
4. Stir in the ground beef with seasoning. Let them cook for 5 min. Stir in the tomato paste with hot water.
5. Let them cook for an extra 6 min to make the sauce.
6. Get a mixing bowl: Combine in it the cottage cheese with eggs well.
7. Spread some of the meat sauce in the bottom of a greased casserole dish.
8. Place over it half of the pasta. Spread over it the cheese mix followed by half of the mozzarella cheese and half of the meat sauce.
9. Cover them with the remaining pasta. Spread the remaining meat sauce on top followed by the remaining mozzarella cheese.
10. Sprinkle the parmesan cheese on top. Place the lasagna in the oven and let it cook for 32 min.
11. Allow the lasagna to sit for 6 min then serve it.
12. Enjoy.

Seattle Café Tofu Spring Rolls

Prep Time: 1 h
Total Time: 1 h

Servings per Recipe: 24
Calories   65.8
Fat   3.1g
Cholesterol   0.2m g
Sodium   160.6mg
Carbohydrates   7.6g
Protein   3.1g

Ingredients

Spicy Peanut Sauce
6 tbsp creamy peanut butter
3/4 C. hoisin sauce
1/2 C. lime juice
1/2 - 3/4 tsp cayenne pepper
Spring rolls
1/2 C. minced scallion
1/4 C. chopped basil
1/4 C. chopped cilantro
1/4 C. chopped of mint
16 oz. seasoned tofu, diced
3 C. peeled seeded and chopped cucumbers
3 C. peeled and grated carrots
3 C. shredded Napa cabbage
55 - 60 sheets rice paper, discs 8 - inches across
4 oz. chives

Directions

1. To prepare the dipping sauce:
2. Get a small mixing bowl: Whisk in it all the ingredients.
3. To make the rolls:
4. Get a mixing bowl: Mix in it the scallion with basil, cilantro, mint, tofu, cucumbers, carrots, cabbage, a pinch of salt and pepper.
5. Get filled bowl with hot water. Pick up rice sheet paper. Dip half of it gently into the hot water. Drain it right away.
6. Turn it gently and dip the other half in the water until softens. Gently place it on a damp kitchen towel.
7. Repeat the process with several more rice sheet papers. Pour 1/4 C. of the filling on the side of rice sheet.
8. Bring the sides to the middle then roll it over the filling. Lay the roll on a plate with the seam facing down.
9. Repeat the process with the remaining filling and rice sheets. Cover them tightly with a piece of plastic wrap.
10. Place the rolls plate in the fridge for at 5 h only.
11. Bring a large pot of water to a boil over high heat. Cook in it each rice rolls for 9 to 10 min.
12. Use a scallion or chives to tie the rice rolls. Place them on a serving plate.
13. Serve them right away with your favorite dipping sauce.
14. Enjoy.

ARTISANAL
Broccoli Dinner

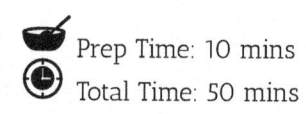

Prep Time: 10 mins
Total Time: 50 mins

Servings per Recipe: 8
Calories   388.7
Fat   24.5g
Cholesterol   46.8mg
Sodium   665.8mg
Carbohydrates   36.2g
Protein   10.9g

Ingredients

3 lbs. broccoli, chopped broccoli
1/4 C. butter
1/4 C. flour
1 1/2 tbsp chicken stock powder
1/2 tsp salt
2 C. milk
6 tbsp butter
2/3 C. coarsely chopped walnuts

0.667 (8 ounce) packages herb seasoned stuffing mix
2/3 C. hot water

Directions

1. Bring a large pot of salted water to a boil. Cook in it the broccoli for 5 to 6 min. Drain it.
2. Place a heavy saucepan over medium heat. Combine in it 1/4 C. butter, flour, chicken stock base, and salt. Mix them well.
3. Add the milk and combine them well. Turn off the heat and place the sauce aside.
4. Get a mixing bowl: Mix in it 6 tbsp of butter with 2/3 C. of hot water and seasoning packet.
5. Get a mixing bowl: Stir in it water mix with the stuffing. Mix in it the chopped nuts.
6. Grease a casserole dish. Place in it the broccoli in an even layer. Spread over it the stuffing followed by the milk sauce.
7. Place the casserole in the oven. Let it cook for 22 to 26 min.
8. Serve your broccoli casserole warm.
9. Enjoy.

Pine Chicken Rolls

Prep Time: 20 mins
Total Time: 40 mins

Servings per Recipe: 6
Calories 410.7
Fat 27.4g
Cholesterol 106.9mg
Sodium 211.2mg
Carbohydrates 4.1g
Protein 36.8g

Ingredients

- 6 chicken breasts, boneless skinless
- 6 slices prosciutto
- 1 (10 ounce) boxes frozen spinach, defrosted
- 3 tbsp pine nuts
- 1/2 C. ricotta cheese
- 1/4 C. parmesan cheese, grated
- 2 garlic cloves, chopped
- 1 tsp nutmeg
- 3 tbsp olive oil, extra virgin
- salt and pepper

Directions

1. Before you do anything, preheat the oven to 400 F.
2. Press the spinach in a kitchen towel to dry it.
3. Place a pan over medium heat. Melt some butter in a pan. Toast in it the pine nuts until they become golden. Drain them.
4. Get a mixing bowl: Toss in it the pinenuts with spinach, cheese, garlic, salt, pepper and nutmeg to make the filling.
5. Use a sharp knife to make a long slit on the side of the chicken breasts without cutting them all the way. Butterfly style.
6. Place the chicken breasts on a lined up baking sheet. Stuff each breasts with some of the spinach filling.
7. Use toothpicks to seal them. Sprinkle over them some salt and pepper.
8. Place the stuffed chicken breasts in the oven and let them cook for 19 to 22 min or until they are done.
9. Serve your stuffed chicken breasts warm with some rice.
10. Enjoy.

ARTISANAL
French Onion Soup

Prep Time: 30 mins
Total Time: 2 h 30 mins

Servings per Recipe: 6
Calories   429.2
Fat   19.4g
Cholesterol   44.1mg
Sodium   2840.4mg
Carbohydrates   39.5g
Protein   13.1g

Ingredients

3 - 3 1/2 lbs. onions, peeled and sliced
0.667 (749 5/8 ml) bottles Riesling wine
6 (12 ounce) cans beef broth
1/2 C. butter
3 tbsp Worcestershire sauce
2 tbsp garlic
2 tbsp paprika
2 bay leaves

2/3 C. flour
salt
French bread
cheddar cheese

Directions

1. Place a pot over medium heat. Heat in it the butter until it melts. Cook in it the onion with garlic for 4 min.
2. Add the salt, pepper, paprika, Worcestershire and bay leafs. Cook them for 1 min.
3. Stir in the broth with wine. Cook them over high heat until they start boiling.
4. Get a mixing bowl: Whisk in it 1 can of broth with flour until no lumps are found.
5. Stir the flour broth back into the pot. Lower the heat and let them cook for 60 min to 120 min.
6. Adjust the seasoning of the soup. Serve it hot with some bread and cheddar cheese.
7. Enjoy.

Rachel's Rasp Pie

Prep Time: 20 mins
Total Time: 50 mins

Servings per Recipe: 8
Calories   408.1
Fat   23.5g
Cholesterol   53.9mg
Sodium   189.7mg
Carbohydrates   47.2g
Protein   4.2g

Ingredients

- 9 inches pie shells, baked & cooled
- 6 oz. cream cheese, softened
- 1/2 C. confectioners' sugar
- 1/4 tsp vanilla extract
- 3/4 C. heavy whipping cream, whipped until stiff peaks are formed
- 2/3 C. granulated sugar
- 1/4 C. cornstarch
- 1/2 C. water
- 1/4 C. lemon juice
- 4 C. raspberries

Directions

1. Before you do anything, preheat the oven to 350 F.
2. Get a mixing bowl: Combine in it the soft cream cheese, confectioner sugar and vanilla with an electric mixer until they become creamy.
3. Stir in the rest of the cream gently to make the filling.
4. Spoon the filling into a pie shell in an even layer.
5. Place a heavy saucepan over medium heat. Stir in it the sugar, cornstarch, water and lemon juice.
6. Add the raspberries and cook them over medium heat and 3 min until they pop and sauce becomes thick.
7. Get a mixing bowl: Place over it a mesh sieve. Pour in it the raspberry sauce and strain it.
8. Press the raspberries with the back of spoon to drain it. Place the strained sauce in the fridge until it cools down completely.
9. Pour the sauce over the cream layer and spread it. Place the pie in the fridge and let it chill for at least 1 h in the fridge.
10. Garnish your pie with your favorite toppings.
11. Enjoy.

PACIFIC
Ocean Pie

🥣 Prep Time: 45 mins
⏱ Total Time: 1 h 45 mins

Servings per Recipe: 8
Calories 681.0
Fat 49.8g
Cholesterol 234.9mg
Sodium 317.4mg
Carbohydrates 53.8g
Protein 7.7g

Ingredients

Pie Shell
1 1/4 C. unbleached all-purpose flour
1/2 tsp salt
1 1/2 tsp granulated sugar
1/3 C. sweetened flaked coconut
8 tbsp unsalted butter, cut into pieces and frozen for 10 minutes
1 1/2 tbsp sour cream
2 tbsp ice water
Insides
1 (13 1/2 ounce) cans coconut milk, well stirred
1 C. whole milk
1/2 C. sweetened flaked coconut
1 vanilla bean, split

2/3 C. granulated sugar, divided
1/4 tsp salt
5 large egg yolks
1/4 C. cornstarch
1/2 tsp coconut extract
2 tbsp unsalted butter, cut into pieces
Garnish
1 1/2 C. heavy whipping cream, chilled
1 1/2 tbsp granulated sugar
1/2 tsp vanilla extract
1 1/2 tsp dark rum
1/4 C. sweetened flaked coconut, toasted
1 ounce white chocolate, shaved

Directions

1. To prepare the pie crust:
2. Get a food processor: Combine in it the flour, salt, sugar and coconut. Pulse them several times.
3. Mix in the butter then pulse them several times until they become coarse.
4. Get a small mixing bowl: Stir in it the sour cream with ice water. Add half of the mixture to the flour mix.
5. Pulse them several times to blend them smooth. Add the rest of the cream mix.
6. Blend them smooth while adding more icy water if the dough it too thick.
7. Shape the dough into 4 inches thick circles. Cover them completely with a plastic wrap. Place them in the fridge for 60 to 120 min.
8. Before you do anything, preheat the oven to 350 F.
9. Once the time is up, allow the dough stick to sit for a while.
10. Place the dough balls on a floured surface. Roll the dough into a 9 inches crust.
11. Place a heavy saucepan over medium heat. Combine in it the coconut milk, milk, coconut,

vanilla bean, 1/3 C. sugar and salt.
12. Bring the mixture to a simmer.
13. Get a mixing bowl. Whisk in it the egg yolks until they become pale.
14. Add the remaining 1/3 C. sugar and cornstarch. Whisk them until no lumps are found.
15. Ladle some of the hot milk mix into the bowl. Mix them until they become smooth.
16. Add the mixture back into the saucepan. Let the sauce cook until it becomes thick for about 40 sec to make the filling.
17. Add the butter with vanilla extract to the filling. Stir them well.
18. Pour the filling into the pie crust. Place it in the fridge and let it sit for at least 4 h.
19. Garnish your pie with your favorite toppings then serve it.
20. Enjoy.

COUNTRY
Cobbler With Streusel

Prep Time: 20 mins
Total Time: 1 h 20 mins

Servings per Recipe: 8
Calories   474.2
Fat   22.2g
Cholesterol   30.5mg
Sodium   239.6mg
Carbohydrates   66.0g
Protein   5.1g

Ingredients
Insides
3 C. strawberries, hulled and sliced
3 C. rhubarb, sliced
3/4 C. granulated sugar
1 tsp orange zest
2 tsp lemon juice
1/4 tsp vanilla extract
1 dash allspice
4 tbsp quick-cooking tapioca

2 tbsp unsalted butter, diced
1 nine-inch pie crust, unbaked
Streusel
1 C. flour
1/3 C. brown sugar
1/4 tsp salt
1/4 tsp nutmeg
6 tbsp unsalted butter, cold and diced
1/2 C. sliced almonds, toasted

Directions
1. Before you do anything, preheat the oven to 400 F.
2. Place the pie crust in a pie pan.
3. To make the filling:
4. Get a mixing bowl: Stir in it the strawberries, rhubarb, sugar, orange zest, lemon juice, vanilla, allspice and tapioca. Let them sit for 6 min.
5. To make the Streusel:
6. Get a blender: Combine in it the flour with brown sugar, nutmeg and salt. Pulse them several times to mix them.
7. Mix in the almonds with and pulse them again until they become chopped.
8. Spoon the strawberry filling into the crust. Top it with the diced butter. Sprinkle the streusel on top.
9. Place the tart in the oven and let it cook for 26 min. Remove it from the oven.
10. Lower the oven heat to 350 F. Use a strip of foil to cover the edge of the pie crust.
11. Let it cook for an extra 42 to 46 min. Allow the tart to cool down for at least 3 h.
12. Garnish the tart with your some whipping cream then serve it.
13. Enjoy.

Asian Soba Salad

Prep Time: 15 mins
Total Time: 25 mins

Servings per Recipe: 8
Calories   420.9
Fat   18.3g
Cholesterol   0.0mg
Sodium   1466.4mg
Carbohydrates   56.5g
Protein   14.1g

Ingredients

16 oz. soba noodles
1/4 C. dark sesame oil
1 tsp dark sesame oil
1/2 C. soy sauce
1/4 C. sugar
1/4 C. tahini

2 tbsp rice wine vinegar
cayenne pepper
1 bunch green onion, sliced
1/2 C. toasted sesame seeds

Directions

1. Prepare the pasta by following the instructions on the package until it becomes dente. Drain it.
2. Get a mixing bowl: Stir in it the noodles with 1 tsp of sesame oil.
3. Place a saucepan over low heat. Stir in it the sugar with soy sauce. Let them cook for 11 min while stirring them.
4. Get a mixing bowl: Combine in it the tahini, 1/4 C. sesame oil, vinegar, water, a pinch of salt and pepper.
5. Mix in the sugar sauce. Combine them well to make the dressing.
6. Add the dressing to the noodles with sesame seeds and green onions. Toss them to coat.
7. Adjust the seasoning of your noodles salad then serve it.
8. Enjoy.

HILLMAN
Café Potato Soup

Prep Time: 21 mins
Total Time: 6 h 21 mins

Servings per Recipe: 8
Calories   357.8
Fat   10.1g
Cholesterol   22.4mg
Sodium   857.8mg
Carbohydrates   55.3g
Protein   13.6g

Ingredients

6 large russet potatoes, peeled and cubed
1 large yellow onion, chopped
42 oz. organic low sodium chicken broth
1 whole garlic clove, smashed with the back of your knife
1/4 C. butter
2 tsp salt
1 1/4 tsp ground pepper
1 C. fat-free half-and-half milk
1 C. shredded reduced-fat sharp cheddar cheese
3 tbsp chopped chives
1 C. light sour cream
4 slices bacon, crisp and crumbled
shredded cheddar cheese

Directions

1. Stir the potato with onion, broth, garlic, butter, salt and pepper.
2. Put on the lid and let them cook for 6 h on high or 10 h on low.
3. Once the time is up, use a potato masher to mash the potato until they become smooth.
4. Add the cheese with chives, half and half, a pinch of salt and pepper.
5. Spoon your potato soup into serving bowl. Garnish them with sour cream.
6. Enjoy.

Feta Artichoke Salad

🥣 Prep Time: 15 mins
🕐 Total Time: 25 mins

Servings per Recipe: 6
Calories   ≈ 750
Fat   607.1
Cholesterol   35.1g
Sodium   71.4mg
Carbohydrates   1593.1mg
Protein   54.6g

Ingredients

- 18 -19 oz. cheese tortellini
- 8 oz. good quality feta cheese, cubed
- 1 C. pitted black olives, broken into pieces
- 1/2 C. sliced green onion
- 1 (15 ounce) cans artichokes, drained & chopped
- 2/3 C. slivered almonds, toasted
- 2 tsp lemon zest
- 1/4 C. lemon juice
- 1/3 C. extra virgin olive oil
- 1 tsp sea salt
- 1/4 tsp ground black pepper
- 1/2 tsp dried oregano

Directions

1. Prepare the tortellini by following the instructions on the package. Run it under some cool water then drain it.
2. Get a mixing bowl: Mix in it the lemon zest, juice, olive oil, salt, pepper and oregano to make the dressing.
3. Get a mixing bowl: Combine the tortellini with feta cheese, olives, green onions, and artichoke hearts.
4. Drizzle the dressing on top then stir them to coat.
5. Place the salad in the fridge and let it sit for at least 30 min.
6. Garnish it with the toasted almonds then serve it.
7. Enjoy.

NEW HOLLY
Pilaf

Prep Time: 10 mins
Total Time: 40 mins

Servings per Recipe: 6
Calories   246.4
Fat   5.4g
Cholesterol   0.0mg
Sodium   326.1mg
Carbohydrates   42.5g
Protein   6.7g

Ingredients
2 1/2 C. low sodium chicken broth
1/8 tsp saffron
1 tbsp extra virgin olive oil
1 medium yellow onion, small diced
1 red bell pepper, cored, seeded, and diced
1 1/2 C. long-grain white rice
1 tsp kosher salt

1/8 tsp cayenne pepper
1/4 C. chopped parsley, divided
1 large garlic clove, minced
1/4 C. slivered almonds, toasted
1 tbsp oregano, chopped

Directions
1. Place a large saucepan over medium heat. Heat in it the broth. Stir in the saffron. Put on the lid and let rest for 18 to 22 min.
2. Place a large saucepan over heat. Heat in it the oil. Cook in it the bell pepper with onion for 5 min.
3. Stir the rice with salt and cayenne pepper. Let them cook for 6 min.
4. Add the garlic with 2 tbsp of parsley and saffron broth. Cook them until they start boiling. Cook them until they start boiling.
5. Put on the lid and lower the heat. Let them cook for 20 min. Turn off the heat and let the rice pilaf rest with the lid on for 6 min.
6. Once the time is up, stir in the almonds with remaining parsley and oregano.
7. Adjust the seasoning of your pilaf the serve it warm.
8. Enjoy.

Onion Soup Stroganoff

Prep Time: 10 mins
Total Time: 1 h 40 mins

Servings per Recipe: 6
Calories	333.2
Fat	5.2g
Cholesterol	63.8mg
Sodium	567.1mg
Carbohydrates	60.1g
Protein	11.9g

Ingredients

- 3 lbs. cubed round steaks
- 1 - 1 1/2 lb. egg noodles
- 2 (10 3/4 ounce) cans mushroom soup
- 1 C. mushrooms, sliced
- 1.5 (1 1/3 ounce) envelopes onion soup mix
- 3/4 C. water

Directions

1. Before you do anything, preheat the oven to 350 F.
2. Place an ovenproof pan over medium heat. Heat in it a splash of oil.
3. Cook in it the steaks dices for 6 min. Stir in the mushroom soup, onion soup mix, water, a pinch of salt and pepper.
4. Place the pan in the oven. Let it cook for 100 min.
5. Prepare the noodles by following the instructions on the package.
6. Once the time is up, serve your steak stew warm noodles.
7. Enjoy.

CITRUS
Chicken Thighs with Seattle Cream Glaze

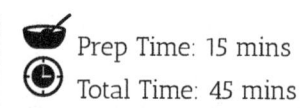

🥣 Prep Time: 15 mins
🕐 Total Time: 45 mins

Servings per Recipe: 4
Calories 555.2
Fat 40.8g
Cholesterol 157.9mg
Sodium 1025.9mg
Carbohydrates 13.4g
Protein 35.3g

Ingredients

- 4 large poblano peppers
- 1 large lime
- 1/2 C. Mexican crema
- 2 tbsp chopped cilantro
- 2 tsp kosher salt, more
- 1 tbsp ground coriander
- 1 tsp ground cumin
- 1/2 tsp ground black pepper
- 8 medium chicken thighs, bone-in & skin-on, trimmed
- 3 tbsp extra virgin olive oil

Directions

1. Before you do anything, preheat the oven broiler on high.
2. Place the rack 5 inches away from the heat source and cover it with a large piece of foil.
3. Lay the poblano peppers over the foil sheet and let them cook for 13 to 16 min until they become black but not burnt.
4. Flip them every 5 min. Place the peppers in a bowl and cover it. Let them sit for 6 min
5. Once the time is up, peel the peppers and dice them.
6. Slice the lime is half. Slice one half into wedges. Squeeze the other half to get 2 tsp of juice.
7. Get a mixing bowl: Mix in it the sour cream with lime juice and cilantro. Add the diced peppers and toss them to coat.
8. Get a mixing bowl: Mix in it 2 tsp of salt with coriander, cumin, and pepper.
9. Brush the chicken thighs with oil then rub them with the spice mix.
10. Place them on a lined up baking tray. Place them in the oven and let them cook for 8 to 11 min. Flip the chicken thighs and cook them for an extra 5 to 7 min.
11. Place the chicken thighs on a serving plate. Top them with the poblano pepper salsa.
12. Serve them warm with some rice.
13. Enjoy.

Simple Torta

Prep Time: 15 mins
Total Time: 8 h 15 mins

Servings per Recipe: 16
Calories   187.0
Fat   14.9g
Cholesterol   39.1mg
Sodium   316.1mg
Carbohydrates   2.8g
Protein   11.0g

Ingredients

- 1/2 C. prepared basil pesto
- 1/2 C. bottled roasted red pepper, drained, rinsed, chopped
- 28 oz. mild goat cheese, softened
- vegetable oil cooking spray

Directions

1. Pour the pesto in a mesh sieve. Drain it and place it aside. Discard the strained oil.
2. Use some paper towels to remove some of the excess liquid from the peppers. Dice them
3. Grease a casserole dish. Cover it with a large piece of plastic wrap.
4. Pour 1/3 of the cheese in the lined up casserole. Spread it in an even layer. Spread over it the pesto sauce.
5. Lay half of the remaining cheese on top. Lay the diced peppers on top in an even layer. Cover it with the rest of the cheese.
6. Lay gently a piece of plastic wrap on top of the cheese to cover it. Press it down gently.
7. Place the dip casserole in the fridge and let it sit for 9 h or more.
8. Once the time is up, discard the plastic sheet. Transfer the dip to a serving dish.
9. Serve it with some bread, crackers, bread sticks or nachos.
10. Enjoy.

SEATTLE
Mushroom Gratin

🥣 Prep Time: 30 mins
🕐 Total Time: 55 mins

Servings per Recipe: 8
Calories   356.3
Fat   26.1g
Cholesterol   75.9mg
Sodium   605.1mg
Carbohydrates   21.2g
Protein   12.9g

Ingredients

9 tbsp unsalted butter
1 (1 lb.) bag frozen pearl onions, thawed and drained
3 lbs. assorted mushrooms, trimmed and halved
3/4 C. heavy cream
1 C. grated parmesan cheese
1 tsp salt
1/4 tsp ground pepper
1 C. coarse plain breadcrumbs

Directions

1. Before you do anything, preheat the oven to 350 F.
2. Place an oven proof pan over medium heat. Heat in it the butter until it melts.
3. Cook in it the onion for 6 min. Drain it and place it aside.
4. Heat 2 tbsp of butter in the same pan. Cook in it 1/4 of the mushroom for 6 min. Drain it and add it to the onion.
5. Do the same thing for the rest of the mushroom.
6. Drain it and add it to the onion. Mix in the heavy cream, 1/2 C. Parmesan, salt, and pepper.
7. Pour the mixture into the cooking pan. Top it with the breadcrumbs and 1/2 C. of parmesan cheese.
8. Place the pan in the oven and let it cook for 26 min.
9. Serve your cream mushroom pan hot with some rice or noodles.
10. Enjoy.

Cheesy Asparagus

Prep Time: 15 mins
Total Time: 15 mins

Servings per Recipe: 6
Calories   162.6
Fat   11.4g
Cholesterol   26.5mg
Sodium   143.0mg
Carbohydrates   8.6g
Protein   8.9g

Ingredients

Spears
2 lbs. asparagus
garlic powder
salt
pepper
olive oil
Sauce

4 oz. goat cheese
2/3 C. sour cream
1/4 C. buttermilk
1/2 C. basil
1 garlic clove
butter

Directions

1. To make the asparagus:
2. Before you do anything, preheat the oven grill and grease it.
3. Trim the asparagus spears and coat them with oil. Place them on the grill.
4. Sprinkle over them some garlic powder, salt and pepper.
5. Let them cook for few minutes until they become tender to your liking.
6. To make the sauce:
7. Get a blender: Combine in it the goat cheese, sour cream, butter milk, and basil. Blend them smooth.
8. Place a small pan over medium heat. Heat in it the butter until it melts.
9. Cook in it the garlic for 45 sec. Add to it the cheese mixture and stir them well.
10. Drizzle the sauce all over the asparagus spears then serve them warm.
11. Enjoy.

SCALLOPED
Potatoes in Seattle

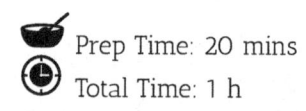

Prep Time: 20 mins
Total Time: 1 h

Servings per Recipe: 10
Calories   253.6
Fat   18.1g
Cholesterol   41.5mg
Sodium   607.7mg
Carbohydrates   17.3g
Protein   6.2g

Ingredients

1/2 C. butter
1/2 C. chopped yellow onion
1 (10 3/4 ounce) cans condensed cream of mushroom soup
16 - 20 oz. chunk-style frozen hash brown potatoes, thawed
1/2 tsp salt
1/4 tsp pepper
1 1/4 C. milk

1 small green bell pepper, strips
1 C. sharp cheddar cheese, grated
2 tbsp chopped pimiento
1 1/4 C. crumbled cheese crackers, divided

Directions

1. Before you do anything, preheat the oven to 375 F.
2. Place a pan over medium heat. Heat in it the butter. Cook in it the onion for 6 min.
3. Get a mixing bowl: Whisk in it the soup with milk.
4. Stir in the potatoes, onions, cheese, peppers, pimentos, salt and pepper, and 1/2 C. of the cracker crumbs.
5. Pour the mixture into a greased casserole dish. Sprinkle over it the remaining cracker crumb.
6. Place the casserole in the oven. Let it cook for 36 to 42 min.
7. Serve your potato casserole warm.
8. Enjoy.

Shortbread Cookies

Prep Time: 25 mins
Total Time: 35 mins

Servings per Recipe: 24
Calories   147.7
Fat   10.1g
Cholesterol   29.9mg
Sodium   117.6mg
Carbohydrates   8.1g
Protein   5.8g

Ingredients
- 4 C. grated sharp cheddar cheese
- 1/2 C. unsalted butter, cubed
- 1 1/2 tbsp Old Bay Seasoning
- 2 C. unbleached white flour

Directions
1. Before you do anything, preheat the oven to 400 F.
2. Get a blender: Combine in it the cheese, butter, and Old Bay Seasoning. Blend them smooth.
3. Add the flour gradually while blending them until you get a smooth dough.
4. Form the dough into a ball. Place it on a floured board and flatten it until it becomes 1/4 inch.
5. Use a cookie cutter to the dough into circles. Lay them on a lined up baking sheet.
6. Place the cookies in the oven and let them cook for 11 min until they become golden.
7. Allow the cookies to cool down completely then serve them.
8. Enjoy.

ROXY'S
Apple Bites

Prep Time: 10 mins
Total Time: 15 mins

Servings per Recipe: 8
Calories   240.8
Fat   0.1g
Cholesterol   0.0mg
Sodium   2.3mg
Carbohydrates   62.5g
Protein   0.2g

Ingredients
4 medium apples, cored and sliced into rings
2 C. sugar
1 C. water
1/3 C. red cinnamon candies
red food coloring

Directions
1. Place a heavy saucepan over medium heat. Stir in it the sugar, water, and candies until they melt.
2. Lower the heat and add few drops of food coloring.
3. Stir in the apple slices and let them cook until they become soft. Test them with a fork.
4. Drain the apple rings and place them on a serving plate.
5. Let them cool down for few minutes. Serve them with some ice cream, pie or cake.
6. Enjoy.

Martha Washington Pops

Prep Time: 10 mins
Total Time: 4 h 10 mins

Servings per Recipe: 16
Calories   18.4
Fat   0.0g
Cholesterol   0.0mg
Sodium   147.9mg
Carbohydrates   1.7g
Protein   2.9g

Ingredients
1 (3 ounce) packages sugar-free Jell-O
1 (1 1/3 ounce) packages sugar-free Kool-Aid mix
2 C. boiling water
cold water

Directions
1. Get a large measuring C. Stir in it all the ingredients.
2. Add enough cold water to them until they make 2 quarts.
3. Pour the mixture into popsicle molds. Freeze them for at least 4 h.
4. Serve your Jell-O pops in a hot day.
5. Enjoy.

VIETNAMESE
Pho I
(Rice Noodle Soup)

Prep Time: 10 mins
Total Time: 1 h 30 mins

Servings per Recipe: 8
Calories   528 kcal
Carbohydrates   73.1 g
Cholesterol   51 mg
Fat   13.6 g
Fiber   3.9 g
Protein   27.1 g
Sodium   2844 mg

Ingredients

4 quarts beef broth
1 large onion, sliced into rings
6 slices fresh ginger root
1 lemon grass
1 cinnamon stick
1 tsp whole black peppercorns
1 pound sirloin tip, cut into thin slices
1/2 pound bean sprouts
1 cup fresh basil leaves
1 cup fresh mint leaves

1 cup loosely packed cilantro leaves
3 fresh jalapeno peppers, sliced into rings
2 limes, cut into wedges
2 (8 ounce) packages dried rice noodles
1/2 tbsp hoisin sauce
1 dash hot pepper sauce
3 tbsps fish sauce

Directions

1. Bring the mixture of broth, onion, lemon grass, cinnamon, ginger and peppercorns to boil before turning down the heat to low and cooking it for about one hour.
2. Place bean sprouts, basil, cilantro, chilies, mint and lime on a platter very neatly.
3. Place noodles in hot water for about 15 minutes before placing it in six different bowls evenly.
4. Put raw beef over it before pouring in hot broth.
5. Serve it with the platter and sauces.

Full Macaroni Salad in Seattle

Prep Time: 10 mins
Total Time: 20 mins

Servings per Recipe: 8
Calories   380.2
Fat   14.4g
Cholesterol   20.6mg
Sodium   677.0mg
Carbohydrates   51.1g
Protein   11.4g

Ingredients

- 1 lb. elbow macaroni
- 3/4 C. mayonnaise
- 2 tbsp white vinegar
- 1 tbsp Dijon mustard
- 1 tbsp sugar
- 1 tsp salt
- 1/4 tsp black pepper
- 1/2 red bell pepper, seeded and small diced
- 1 (3 7/8 ounce) cans sliced black olives
- 4 oz. medium cheddar, cubed

Directions

1. Prepare the pasta by following the instructions on the package.
2. Get a mixing bowl: Mix in it the mayonnaise, vinegar, mustard, sugar, salt and pepper.
3. Stir in the bell pepper, olives and cheese. Add the macaroni and toss them to coat.
4. Chill the salad in the fridge for at least 3 h then serve it.
5. Enjoy.

CHERRY CAPRESE
Kabobs with Lemon Dressing

Prep Time: 15 mins
Total Time: 15 mins

Servings per Recipe: 6
Calories	283.8
Fat	26.5g
Cholesterol	29.8mg
Sodium	433.8mg
Carbohydrates	3.3g
Protein	8.9g

Ingredients
8 oz. mozzarella cheese
1 pint cherry tomatoes
Dressing
1/2 C. extra virgin olive oil
1 tbsp squeezed lemon juice
5 tbsp chopped basil

1 large garlic clove, minced
1/2 tsp salt
1/4 tsp ground black pepper

Directions
1. Get a mixing bowl: Mix in it all the dressing ingredients.
2. Thread the mozzarella cheese pieces and cherry tomatoes into wooden skewers while alternating between them.
3. Drizzle the vinaigrette over the Caprese skewers. Serve your salad right away.
4. Enjoy.

Alaskan Salmon Dip

Prep Time: 10 mins
Total Time: 1 h 10 mins

Servings per Recipe: 6
Calories   93.4
Fat   6.5g
Cholesterol   32.0mg
Sodium   250.0mg
Carbohydrates   0.8g
Protein   7.6g

Ingredients

- 1 (7 ounce) cans salmon
- 1/4 C. cream cheese
- 1/4 C. sour cream
- 2 tbsp green onions, chopped
- 1 tbsp dill, chopped
- 1 tsp vinegar
- 1/2 tsp salt
- 1 pinch pepper

Directions

1. Get a mixing bowl: Mix in it the cream cheese with salmon until they become smooth.
2. Add the sour cream, green onion, dill, vinegar, salt, and pepper. Combine them well.
3. Place the dip in the fridge for at least 1 h. Serve it with some veggies sticks or crackers.
4. Enjoy.

ALTERNATIVE
Blackberry Crisp (Slump)

Prep Time: 10 mins
Total Time: 45 mins

Servings per Recipe: 4
Calories   637.1
Fat   13.6g
Cholesterol   34.8mg
Sodium   307.6mg
Carbohydrates   127.1g
Protein   6.3g

Ingredients
- 1 quart blackberry, washed and stemmed
- 1 1/2 C. sugar
- 1 1/2 tsp baking powder
- 1 C. all-purpose flour
- 1/2 C. milk
- 1/8 tsp salt
- 4 tbsp sugar
- 4 tbsp melted butter

Directions
1. Before you do anything, preheat the oven to 375 F.
2. Toss 1 1/2 C. of sugar with the berries. Place it aside.
3. Get a mixing bowl: Mix in it the baking powder with flour, milk, salt, 4 tbsp of sugar and butter.
4. Pour the batter all over the berries layer. Place the pan in the oven.
5. Let the tart cook for 46 min.
6. Allow the berry tart too cool down completely. Serve it with some whipping cream or ice cream.
7. Enjoy.

Seattle Late-September Muffins

Prep Time: 40 mins
Total Time: 1 h 5 mins

Servings per Recipe: 1
Calories   280.8
Fat   11.4g
Cholesterol   39.6mg
Sodium   228.2mg
Carbohydrates   41.8g
Protein   3.5g

Ingredients

Muffin
- 24 oz. all-purpose flour
- 2 tsp baking soda
- 23 oz. granulated sugar
- 1/2 tbsp cinnamon
- 1/2 tsp nutmeg
- 1 tsp salt
- 18 oz. canned pumpkin
- 2/3 C. water
- 1 C. vegetable oil
- 4 eggs

Insides
- 12 oz. cream cheese, softened
- 1/4 C. granulated sugar
- 1 dash salt
- 1 egg
- 1/4 tsp vanilla extract

Garnish
- 1 C. brown sugar
- 1 tsp cinnamon
- 4 tbsp butter, melted
- roasted pumpkin seeds

Directions

1. To make the muffins:
2. Before you do anything, preheat the oven to 350 F.
3. Get a mixing bowl: Mix in it the flour with baking soda, sugar, cinnamon, nutmeg, and salt.
4. Add the eggs gradually followed by the water, oil and pumpkin while mixing them all the time until they become smooth.
5. To make the filling:
6. Get a mixing bowl: Beat in it the cream cheese until it becomes light and smooth. Add to it the sugar with salt.
7. Beat it for 2 min. Add the eggs gradually followed by the vanilla extract. Blend them until they become light and creamy.
8. Place the filling in the fridge and let chill for few minutes.
9. To make the topping:
10. Get a mixing bowl: Mix in it the cinnamon with sugar and butter.
11. Grease a muffin tin. Fill 1/3 of the muffin C. with the batter. Top it with a scoop of the filling.
12. Pour the remaining batter on top cover the filling. Add the topping on top.
13. Place the muffin pan in the oven. Let them cook for 16 to 26 min or until they are done
14. Allow the muffins to cool down completely then serve them.
15. Enjoy.

HOT
Smokie Crescents

Prep Time: 30 mins
Total Time: 40 mins

Servings per Recipe: 48
Calories   75.1
Fat   4.6g
Cholesterol   15.4mg
Sodium   172.8mg
Carbohydrates   5.1g
Protein   3.1g

Ingredients
1 (48 link) packages Little Smokies sausages
2 (8 ounce) packages any brand crescent rolls
1 (12 ounce) containers beaver brand sweet-hot mustard
1 (8 ounce) packages grated sharp cheddar cheese

Directions
1. Before you do anything, preheat the oven to temperature mentioned on the package of the crescent roll pack.
2. Unroll the crescent rolls on a board. Slice each crescent roll into 3 triangles.
3. Place over the rolls some sweet mustard. Top it with some cheese.
4. Place a little smokie on the base of each triangle then roll them. Place them on a lined up baking sheet.
5. Cook them in the oven for 11 to 16 min until they become golden brown.
6. Serve your pigs in blanket with some sweet mustard or ketchup.
7. Enjoy.

Pear Tart with Sugar Crumble Pie

Prep Time: 15 mins
Total Time: 50 mins

Servings per Recipe: 6
Calories	456.4
Fat	21.0g
Cholesterol	30.2mg
Sodium	415.8mg
Carbohydrates	63.9g
Protein	5.8g

Ingredients

4 large ripe pears, peeled & sliced
1/3 C. granulated sugar
1 tbsp cornstarch
1/8 tsp salt
1 unbaked pastry shell
Garnish
1/2 C. shredded cheddar cheese

1/2 C. all-purpose flour
1/4 C. butter, melted
1/4 C. granulated sugar
1/4 tsp salt

Directions

1. Before you do anything, preheat the oven to 425 F.
2. To make the filling:
3. Get a mixing bowl: Toss in it the pears, sugar, cornstarch and salt.
4. To make the topping:
5. Get a mixing bowl: Mix in it all the topping ingredients.
6. Place the pastry shell in a pie pan. Pour in it the filling and spread it in an even layer.
7. Sprinkle the topping mix on top. Place the pie in the oven and let it cook for 26 to 32 min.
8. Allow the pie to sit for 12 min. Serve it slightly warm with some ice cream.
9. Enjoy.

VELVEETA
Tex Noodles

Prep Time: 15 mins
Total Time: 45 mins

Servings per Recipe: 12
Calories   285.7
Fat   13.7g
Cholesterol   61.4mg
Sodium   758.5mg
Carbohydrates   23.7g
Protein   16.8g

Ingredients

- 1 1/2 lbs. ground beef, browned and drained
- 3 C. dry wide egg noodles
- 1/2 lb. Velveeta cheese, cubed
- 1 (10 1/2 ounce) cans tomato soup
- 1 tbsp Worcestershire sauce
- 1 C. ketchup
- 1 C. breadcrumbs

Directions

1. Before you do anything, preheat the oven to 350 F.
2. Stir all the ingredients in a casserole dish.
3. Place it in the oven and let it cook for 32 min.
4. Serve your beef casserole with some noodles or rice.
5. Enjoy.

Sun Dried Pesto Sauce

Prep Time: 20 mins
Total Time: 20 mins

Servings per Recipe: 8
Calories   128.6
Fat   9.3g
Cholesterol   0.0mg
Sodium   201.6mg
Carbohydrates   9.1g
Protein   5.1g

Ingredients
1 C. packed sun-dried tomato
1 C. almonds
1 chili pepper, chopped
1 C. chopped tomato
1/4 C. lime juice
salt

Directions
1. Before you do anything, preheat the oven to 350 F.
2. Get a mixing bowl: Place in it the sundried tomato. Cover it with boiling water and let it sit for 16 min to soften.
3. Spread the almonds on a baking sheet in an even layer. Place it in the oven and let them cook for 9 min.
4. Turn off the heat and let the almonds cool down for a while.
5. Chop the almonds roughly and place them aside.
6. Drain the sundried tomatoes.
7. Get a blender: Combine in it the sundried tomatoes with almonds and the remaining ingredients. Blend them smooth.
8. Pour the dressing into a jar and seal it. Place it in the fridge until ready to serve.
9. You can serve them dressing with a sandwich, grilled meat or a salad.
10. Enjoy.

CHARRED Bass with Jalapeño Salsa

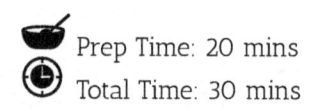

Prep Time: 20 mins
Total Time: 30 mins

Servings per Recipe: 12
Calories 319.4
Fat 2.5g
Cholesterol 46.4mg
Sodium 4487.0mg
Carbohydrates 46.4g
Protein 29.5g

Ingredients

Bass
1 lb. sea bass, cleaned & cut portions
3/4 C. soy sauce
1/2 C. teriyaki sauce
4 oz. brown sugar
vegetable oil
Salsa
1/2 of a pineapple, cleaned & diced
1/2 red bell pepper, diced
1/2 green bell pepper, diced
3 tbsp red onions, diced
1/2 jalapeno, seeded & minced
1/2 C. cilantro, chopped
1/4 C. basil, chiffonade cut
olive oil
salt & pepper

Directions

1. To make the fish:
2. Get a mixing bowl: Whisk in it the soy sauce with teriyaki sauce and brown sugar.
3. Add the sea bass pieces and coat them with the mixture. Let them sit for at least 3 h.
4. To make the pineapple salsa:
5. Get a mixing bowl: Stir in it all the salsa ingredients. Place it in the fridge until ready to serve.
6. Place a large skillet over medium heat. Heat in it 1/8 inch of oil.
7. Cook in it the sea bass fillets for 3 to 5 min on each side until they become golden brown.
8. Serve your sweet bass fillet with some the pineapple salsa and some rice.
9. Enjoy.

Gonzaga Dorm Cookies

Prep Time: 30 mins
Total Time: 37 mins

Servings per Recipe: 1
Calories   73.9
Fat   3.6g
Cholesterol   14.2mg
Sodium   58.4mg
Carbohydrates   9.5g
Protein   0.9g

Ingredients
2/3 C. butter
3/4 C. sugar
1 tsp baking powder
1/4 tsp salt

1 egg
1 tsp vanilla
2 C. flour

Directions
1. Before you do anything, preheat the oven to 375 F.
2. Get a mixing bowl: Whip in it the butter for 35 sec until it becomes light and smooth.
3. Mix in the sugar, baking powder, and salt. Add the eggs with vanilla. Beat them until they become creamy.
4. Add the flour gradually while mixing until you get a soft dough.
5. Cover the dough completely with a piece of plastic wrap. Let it rest for at least 2 h.
6. Transfer the dough to a floured surface. Roll it until it becomes 1/4 inch thick.
7. Use a cookie cutter to cut the dough into your favorite shapes. Place the cookies on a lined up baking sheet.
8. Cook the cookies in the oven for 8 min until they become golden.
9. Allow the cookies to cool down completely then serve them with some tea.
10. Enjoy.

RAINIER
Vista Rollatini

🥣 Prep Time: 30 mins
🕐 Total Time: 1 h 15 mins

Servings per Recipe: 6
Calories 785.9
Fat 39.4g
Cholesterol 283.3mg
Sodium 2322.7mg
Carbohydrates 60.8g
Protein 48.0g

Ingredients

- cooking spray
- 2 large eggplants, unpeeled and sliced lengthwise
- 5 eggs
- 2 -3 C. seasoned breadcrumbs
- 16 oz. part-skim ricotta cheese
- 1/2 C. crumbled feta cheese
- 3/4 C. grated parmesan cheese
- 1 lb. shredded mozzarella cheese
- 3 garlic cloves, minced
- 1/4 C. chopped basil
- 2 tbsp chopped parsley
- salt and pepper
- 26 oz. marinara sauce

Directions

1. Before you do anything, preheat the oven to 375 F.
2. Grease 2 baking trays with a cooking spray or oil.
3. Whisk 3 eggs in a shallow bowl. Place in it the eggplant slices and coat them with.
4. Roll them in the breadcrumbs and lay them on the baking trays. Spray them with a cooking spray.
5. Place the pans in the oven and let them cook for 16 min. Place them aside to cool down.
6. Get a mixing bowl: Combine in it the ricotta, feta, 1/2 C. parmesan, 3 C. mozzarella, remaining two eggs (beaten), garlic, basil, parsley, a pinch of salt and pepper.
7. Grease a baking dish. Spread 1 C. of sauce in the dish. Place 2 tbsp of the filling on an eggplant slice. Roll it over the filling.
8. Place the eggplant roll in the baking dish with the seam facing down.
9. Repeat the process with the remaining filling and eggplant slices. Pour the remaining tomato sauce on top.
10. Sprinkle the mozzarella and parmesan cheese on top. Lay a piece of foil over the dish to cover it.
11. Place it in the oven and let it cook for 32 min.
12. Once the time is up, discard the foil. Let the eggplant casserole cook for an extra 16 min in the oven.
13. Serve it hot with some rice.
14. Enjoy.

Rice Pudding
with Cherry Sauce

Prep Time: 15 mins
Total Time: 1 h 10 mins

Servings per Recipe: 6
Calories 566.2
Fat 38.6g
Cholesterol 124.9mg
Sodium 289.7mg
Carbohydrates 46.2g
Protein 9.9g

Ingredients

Rice
4 C. whole milk
2/3 C. pearl rice
1/2 tsp salt
1 1/2 tsp pure vanilla extract
2 C. heavy whipping cream
1/2 C. granulated sugar
1/2 C. sliced almonds, toasted
Glaze

1 (16 oz.) cans cherries in juice
1 tbsp cornstarch
1/3 C. water

Directions

1. To prepare the rice:
2. Place a large saucepan over medium heat. Heat in it the milk until it starts boiling.
3. Stir in the rice with salt. Put on the lid and let them cook for 52 min over low heat.
4. Once the time is up, turn off the heat. Allow the rice to cool down for 10 min. Cover it with a plastic wrap.
5. Place it in the fridge and let cool down completely.
6. Get a mixing bowl: Beat in it the whipping cream with vanilla and sugar until they become smooth and its stiff peaks.
7. Add the cool rice and fold it into the cream. Cover the pudding and place again in the fridge.
8. To prepare the cherry sauce:
9. Place a heavy saucepan over medium heat. Stir in the cherries with its juice. Cook them until they start boiling.
10. Get a small mixing bowl: Whisk in it the cornstarch with water. Stir them into the cherries pan.
11. Let them cook for 1 to 2 in until they become thick while stirring them all the time.
12. Divide the rice pudding between serving bowls. Spoon the cherry sauce on top then serve them.
13. Enjoy.

HOW TO SMOKE a Turkey

Prep Time: 2 days
Total Time: 61 h

Servings per Recipe: 10
Calories	661.4
Fat	34.6g
Cholesterol	270.9mg
Sodium	11591.2mg
Carbohydrates	0.0g
Protein	81.3g

Ingredients
1 (12 lb.) whole turkey
1 C. pickling salt
2 C. Morton's tender quick
10 tbsp liquid smoke
2 gallons water
2 tbsp vegetable oil

Directions
1. Get a bucket. Mix in it the salt with tender quick, liquid smoke and water. Stir them well to make the brine.
2. Add turkey to the brine. Let it sit for at 25 h to 38 h.
3. Before you do anything, preheat the oven to 350 F.
4. Once the time is up, Drain the turkey and run it under some cool water. Pat it dry.
5. Coat the turkey with some salad oil. Place it in a roasting dish with the breast facing down.
6. Place the turkey pan in the oven. Let it cook for 65 min. Lower the heat to 250 F.
7. Let the turkey cook in it the oven for 12 h.
8. Once the time is up, wrap the turkey in a piece of foil. Let it rest for 4 h then serve it.
9. Enjoy.

Mixed Green Salad with Berry Dressing

🥣 Prep Time: 20 mins
🕐 Total Time: 20 mins

Servings per Recipe: 4
Calories   81.0
Fat   6.8g
Cholesterol   0.0mg
Sodium   0.8mg
Carbohydrates   5.4g
Protein   0.3g

Ingredients

2 C. mixed greens
1/4 C. baby arugula
1 C. pineapple, cut into spears
1/4 red bell pepper, seeds removed, diced
1 tbsp toasted sesame seeds
Vinaigrette
2 tbsp sesame oil
1 tbsp olive oil

1 - 2 tbsp raspberry vinegar
1 tsp chopped garlic sprouts
1 tsp thyme
salt and pepper

Directions

1. Get a shallow serving bowl. Lay in it the arugula with greens.
2. Top them with the pineapple chunks followed by bell pepper and sesame seeds.
3. Get a small mixing bowl: Whisk in it all the vinaigrette ingredients. Drizzle them over the salad
4. Serve your salad right away.
5. Enjoy.

AUTHENTIC
Beef and Broccoli

Prep Time: 35 mins
Total Time: 1 h

Servings per Recipe: 4
Calories   572.3
Fat   9.6g
Cholesterol   0.0mg
Sodium   1441.0mg
Carbohydrates   108.2g
Protein   12.3g

Ingredients

- 2 tbsp cornstarch
- 2 tbsp water
- 1/2 tsp garlic powder
- 1 C. low sodium beef broth
- 2/3 C. reduced sodium soy sauce
- 1 tbsp brown sugar
- 2 tbsp minced ginger
- 2 large minced garlic cloves
- 1 lb. boneless steak, strips
- 2 tbsp vegetable oil, divided
- 2 dashes sesame oil, divided
- 4 -6 C. broccoli florets
- 1 dash salt and pepper,
- 1 medium onion, wedges
- 16 oz. cooked cauliflower rice

Directions

1. To prepare the marinade:
2. Get a mixing bowl: Mix in it the beef broth, soy sauce, brown sugar, ginger, and garlic
3. Add to it the steak strips to the marinade and coat them with it. Let them sit for 40 min.
4. Get a mixing bowl: Whisk in it 2 tbsp cornstarch, 2 tbsp water and 1/2 tsp garlic powder.
5. Drain the steaks stripes and add them to the starch mix. Toss them to coat.
6. Place a pan over medium heat. Heat in it 1 tbsp of oil.
7. Cook in it the steak stripes for 3 to 5 min on each side or until they are done to your liking.
8. Drain the steak stripes and place them aside.
9. Heat another 1 tbsp of oil in the same pan. Cook in it the broccoli with onion for 5 min. Season them with a pinch of salt and pepper.
10. Stir the steak strips back into the pan. Let them cook for an extra 3 min.
11. Serve it warm with some rice.
12. Enjoy.

Seattle Spice Rub

Prep Time: 5 mins
Total Time: 5 mins

Servings per Recipe: 1
Calories	295.6
Fat	8.9g
Cholesterol	0.0mg
Sodium	21082.5mg
Carbohydrates	56.4g
Protein	13.0g

Ingredients

- 2 tbsp sea salt
- 2 tbsp ground cumin
- 2 tbsp hot smoked paprika
- 2 tbsp onion powder
- 1 tbsp garlic powder
- 1 tbsp dried ancho chile powder
- 2 tsp ground black pepper

Directions

1. Get a mixing bowl: Mix in it all the ingredients well.
2. Pour the spice mix into an airtight container. Let sit in a cupboard until ready to use.
3. You can use this spice rub with any kind of meat you desire.
4. Enjoy.

MUSHROOM
Sauce Meatballs

Prep Time: 35 mins
Total Time: 1 h 30 mins

Servings per Recipe: 4	
Calories	849 kcal
Carbohydrates	40.6 g
Cholesterol	38 mg
Fat	55.1 g
Fiber	3.4 g
Protein	44.5 g
Sodium	1920 mg

Ingredients
2 pounds lean ground beef
1/3 C. finely chopped green bell pepper
1/3 C. finely chopped onion
2 eggs
1 1/2 C. Italian-style dry bread crumbs
1/2 tsp salt
1/4 tsp ground black pepper
2 (10.75 oz.) cans condensed golden mushroom soup

1 C. sliced fresh mushrooms
1 C. sour cream
1/2 C. milk
2 tbsps browning sauce
salt to taste
ground black pepper to taste

Directions
1. Set your oven to 375 degrees before doing anything else.
2. Get a bowl, combine evenly: black pepper, beef, salt, green pepper, crumbled bread, whisked eggs, and onion.
3. Form your meatballs and place in a baking dish. Cook for 30 mins in the oven.
4. Get a 2nd bowl, mix: black pepper, soup, salt, mushrooms, browning sauce, milk, and sour cream.
5. Coat meatballs with mushroom mix after 30 mins of baking. Then bake for another 20 mins.
6. Enjoy.

Bonnie's
Black Beans

Prep Time: 20 mins
Total Time: 1 h 20 mins

Servings per Recipe: 4
Calories   41.3
Fat   1.9g
Cholesterol   2.7mg
Sodium   211.5mg
Carbohydrates   5.0g
Protein   1.1g

Ingredients
3 C. of black beans, rinsed and drained
6 C. of chicken broth
1/2 C. of water
water
1/2 tsp black pepper
1/4 tsp salt
2 bacon, slices
1 C. sliced celery
1/2 C. chopped onion

1/2 C. chopped carrot
1/2 tsp dried thyme
1/2 tsp ground cumin
2 garlic cloves, minced

Directions
1. Place a large pot over medium heat. Place in it the beans and cover it with water until it is 2 inches on top of it.
2. Let it sit for at least 8 h. Drain it and add it back to the pot.
3. Add to it the broth with 1/2 C. of water, pepper and salt. Cook them until they start boiling.
4. Lower the heat and let the beans cook for 120 min uncovered over low heat.
5. Place a pan over medium heat. Cook in it the bacon until it becomes crisp. Drain it and crumble it.
6. Cook the celery with onion, carrot, thyme, cumin and garlic in the same pan for 6 min.
7. Stir it into the beans pot. Let them cook for 12 min over low heat.
8. Add the crumbled mixture and toss them to coat. Serve your black beans salsa warm.
9. Enjoy.

SEATTLE
Couscous Salad

Prep Time: 30 mins
Total Time: 30 mins

Servings per Recipe: 6
Calories   317.0
Fat   6.5g
Cholesterol   9.8mg
Sodium   222.9mg
Carbohydrates   53.4g
Protein   12.3g

Ingredients

- 1 1/2 C. couscous
- 1 1/2 C. vegetable stock
- 1/4 tsp cumin
- 1/4 tsp coriander
- 1/4 tsp turmeric
- 1/4 tsp black pepper
- 1/4 tsp oregano
- 1/4 C. cilantro, chopped
- 3 tomatoes, seeded and diced
- 3 garlic cloves, minced
- 1/4 red onion, diced
- 1 carrot, grated
- 1/2 C. frozen corn, thawed
- 1/2 C. frozen peas, thawed
- 1/2 avocado, diced
- 1/2 C. canned chick-peas, drained and rinsed
- 1/2 C. canned black beans, drained and rinsed
- 1/2 C. cheddar cheese, grated

Directions

1. Place a pot over medium heat. Heat in it the stock until it starts boiling. Add the couscous and put on the lid.
2. Let it sit for 10 min. Fluff it with a fork.
3. Get a mixing bowl: Toss in it the remaining ingredients.
4. Add the couscous and stir them well. Adjust the seasoning of your salad then serve it.
5. Enjoy.

Romano Zucchini Boats

Prep Time: 15 mins
Total Time: 35 mins

Servings per Recipe: 4
Calories   368.9
Fat   26.4g
Cholesterol   61.8mg
Sodium   1370.2mg
Carbohydrates   11.4g
Protein   23.0g

Ingredients

- 4 zucchini, cut lengthwise and hollowed out. Chop up the hollowed out portion
- 1/2 lb. Italian turkey sausage
- 1/2 C. Romano cheese
- 2 tbsp pine nuts
- 2 tbsp sun-dried tomatoes
- 1/2 tsp salt

Directions

1. Before you do anything, preheat the oven to 425 F.
2. Place a pan over medium heat. Brown in it the sausages until it becomes crumbled for 5 to 6 min.
3. Stir in the chopped zucchini and cook them for 3 min.
4. Turn off the heat and mix in the cheese, pinenuts, and sundried tomatoes to make the filling.
5. Season the hollowed zucchinis with some salt. Spoon the filling into them then place them in a casserole dish.
6. Place the casserole in the oven and let it cook for 22 min.
7. Serve your stuffed zucchini casserole warm.
8. Enjoy.

SEATTLE BBQ
Sauce for Caterers

Prep Time: 15 mins
Total Time: 1 h 30 mins

Servings per Recipe: 50
Calories	133.0
Fat	0.7g
Cholesterol	1.2mg
Sodium	736.3mg
Carbohydrates	33.0g
Protein	1.2g

Ingredients
- 1 (114 oz.) cans ketchup
- 2 tbsp butter
- 1 large white onion, minced
- 1 tsp crushed red pepper flakes
- 1/2 C. minced garlic
- 1 (12 oz.) bottles unsulphered molasses
- 2 1/2 C. brown sugar, packed
- 2 tbsp liquid smoke
- 3/4 C. white vinegar
- 1 1/2 tbsp cracked black pepper
- 4 tbsp creole seasoning

Directions
1. Place a large pot over medium heat. Heat in it the butter until it melts.
2. Cook in it the onion with garlic and pepper flakes. Cook them for 16 min over low heat.
3. Stir in the rest of the ingredients. Lower the heat and let them cook for 35 min.
4. Spoon the sauce into an airtight container. Place it in the fridge until ready to serve.
5. Enjoy.

Wedding Soup 101

Prep Time: 15 mins
Total Time: 40 mins

Servings per Recipe: 15
Calories	294.9
Fat	13.3g
Cholesterol	47.5mg
Sodium	1113.4mg
Carbohydrates	21.6g
Protein	20.7g

Ingredients

- 12 oz. Italian turkey sausage, rolled into meatballs
- 12 oz. boneless skinless chicken breasts, diced
- 2 tbsp olive oil
- 1/4 C. minced garlic
- 1/2 tsp crushed red pepper flakes
- 1 C. roasted red pepper, diced
- 3 quarts chicken broth
- 4 C. cooked Orzo pasta, al dente
- 8 C. baby spinach leaves
- 1 C. grated Romano cheese
- salt
- pepper

Directions

1. Place a large soup pot over medium heat. Heat in it the oil. Cook in it the meatballs for 4 to 6min.
2. Stir the garlic with red pepper and pepper flakes into the pot.
3. Cook them for 1 to 2 min. Stir in the broth and cook them until they stat boiling over high heat.
4. Stir in the pasta with spinach, a pinch of salt and pepper. Serve your soup hot. Garnish it with some cheese.
5. Enjoy.

APPLE
Aoli

🥣 Prep Time: 5 mins
🕐 Total Time: 5 mins

Servings per Recipe: 1
Calories   2006.0
Fat   223.1g
Cholesterol   186.0mg
Sodium   1234.3mg
Carbohydrates   0.9g
Protein   6.6g

Ingredients
1 large egg
1 C. almond oil
1 tsp apple cider vinegar
1/2 tsp mustard powder
1/8 tsp garlic powder
1/2 tsp sea salt

Directions
1. Get a blender: Place in it the egg and blend it smooth.
2. Add the oil in a steady thin stream while it is blending at the same time until the mix become creamy and thick.
3. Pour in the rest of the ingredients. Blend them smooth.
4. Adjust the seasoning of your mayonnaise then serve it.
5. Enjoy.

Chocolate Cake Brownies

Prep Time: 15 mins
Total Time: 35 mins

Servings per Recipe: 1
Calories   93.8
Fat   0.4g
Cholesterol   0.0mg
Sodium   33.5mg
Carbohydrates   22.6g
Protein   1.5g

Ingredients
2 1/2 medium sized bananas, mashed
1 C. baker's sugar
2/3 C. brown sugar, lightly packed
2 large egg whites
2 tsp vanilla extract
1 C. all-purpose flour
1/4 C. kosher cake crumbs

3/4 C. baking cocoa
1/2 tsp baking powder
1/4 tsp kosher salt

Directions
1. Before you do anything, preheat the oven to 350 F. Coat a cake pan with a cooking spray
2. Get a mixing bowl: Place in it the bananas then mash them until they become smooth.
3. Add the sugars and combine them well. Mix in it the egg whites with vanilla extract.
4. Get a mixing bowl: Stir in it the flour, cake meal, cocoa, baking powder and salt.
5. Add the flour mix to the banana mixture. Mix them well.
6. Spoon the batter into the pan. Place it in the oven and let it cook for 22 to 26 min.
7. Allow the cake to cool down completely. Serve it with your favorite toppings.
8. Enjoy.

LEMONY
Chicken Cutlets

Prep Time: 15 mins
Total Time: 30 mins

Servings per Recipe: 3
Calories	757.9
Fat	53.4g
Cholesterol	268.8mg
Sodium	461.7mg
Carbohydrates	21.4g
Protein	48.6g

Ingredients
6 anchovy fillets
1 small garlic clove
kosher salt & ground black pepper
1 lemon, zest
2 1/2 tbsp lemon juice
7 tbsp extra virgin olive oil
2 eggs

1/2 C. flour
1/8 tsp cayenne
1/8 tsp nutmeg
1 1/4 lbs. chicken breasts
oil

Directions
1. Get a blender: Combine in it the anchovies, garlic, salt, pepper, lemon juice/zest and olive oil. Blend them smooth.
2. Get a mixing bowl: Stir in it the flour with nutmeg and cayenne pepper.
3. Get another mixing bowl: Whisk in it the eggs with breadcrumbs.
4. Sprinkle the some salt and pepper over the chicken breasts. Coat them with the garlic mixture.
5. Place a large pan over medium heat. Heat in it the olive oil.
6. Dust the chicken breasts with the flour mix then dip them in the eggs mix.
7. Place them in the hot pan. Cook them for 3 to 5 min on each side or until they are done to your liking.
8. Serve your chicken breasts warm with some rice or a salad.
9. Enjoy.

Seattle Coffee Stew

🥣 Prep Time: 45 mins
🕒 Total Time: 2 h 22 mins

Servings per Recipe: 1
Calories   289.4
Fat   9.3g
Cholesterol   87.9mg
Sodium   1506.5mg
Carbohydrates   12.6g
Protein   38.6g

Ingredients

- 12 large dried pasilla peppers
- 1 1/4 C. strong black coffee
- 1 (13 3/4 oz.) cans chicken broth
- 1/2 C. chopped onion
- 1 - 2 garlic clove, smashed
- 2 tbsp vegetable oil
- 2 lbs. boneless skinless chicken, cubed
- 1 tbsp chili powder
- 1 tbsp sugar
- 1 tbsp salt
- 1 tbsp masa harina, dissolved in 1/4 C. warm water

Directions

1. Get a mixing bowl: Place in it the chilies and cover them with hot water. Let them sit for 35 min.
2. Drain the chilies. Discard their stems and seeds.
3. Get a blender: Combine in it the broth with coffee and chilies. Blend them smooth.
4. Place a large pot over medium heat. Heat in it the oil. Cook in it the garlic with onion for 3 min.
5. Stir in the chicken cubes and cook them for 4 min. Stir in the broth mixture.
6. Cook them until they start boiling. Lower the heat and let them cook for 60 min.
7. Once the time is up, add the masa harina mixture. Let the chili cook for an extra 8 min.
8. Serve your chili warm with some grated cheese.
9. Enjoy.

HOT DOGS
Seattle Style

Prep Time: 10 mins
Total Time: 20 mins

Servings per Recipe: 4
Calories 480.6
Fat 36.5g
Cholesterol 85.5mg
Sodium 885.4mg
Carbohydrates 26.6g
Protein 11.6g

Ingredients
1/4 C. butter
1 sweet onion, sliced
1 (4 oz.) packages cream cheese
4 hot dogs
4 hot dog buns

spicy brown mustard
sauerkraut

Directions
1. Before you do anything, preheat the grill and grease it.
2. Place over it the hot dogs and cook them for 4 to 5 min.
3. Place a pan over low heat. Heat in it the butter until it melts. Cook in it the onion for 16 min.
4. Stir in the cream cheese and heat it until it becomes soft to make the sauce.
5. Spread half of the cheese sauce inside the dog buns. Place the hot dogs on top then top them with the remaining cheese sauce.
6. Top them with some mustard and sauerkraut.
7. Enjoy.

Seattle Tapenade

Prep Time: 5 mins
Total Time: 15 mins

Servings per Recipe: 1
Calories   855.4
Fat   45.5g
Cholesterol   14.6mg
Sodium   2178.8mg
Carbohydrates   93.2g
Protein   21.7g

Ingredients

- 4 garlic cloves, minced
- 1/2 C. lemon juice
- 6 oz. black olives, drained and pitted
- 6 oz. kalamata olives, drained and pitted
- 1/2 C. parsley
- 4 green onions
- 8 large basil leaves
- 1/2 C. parmesan cheese, grated
- 1/3 C. olive oil
- 1 loaf baguette, sliced

Directions

1. Get a blender: Combine 1/4 C. of lemon juice with the rest of the ingredients. Blend them smooth.
2. Pour in the remaining juice and blend again.
3. Spoon the spread into a serving bowl. Serve it with baguette slices.
4. Enjoy.

ARTISANAL
Chicken Salad

🥣 Prep Time: 15 mins
🕐 Total Time: 55 mins

Servings per Recipe: 4
Calories 570.2
Fat 49.0g
Cholesterol 46.4mg
Sodium 2001.6mg
Carbohydrates 12.2g
Protein 23.4g

Ingredients

Salad
4 chicken breast halves, bone-in & skin-on
extra virgin olive oil
kosher salt
ground black pepper
1/2 lb. asparagus, ends removed, and cut in thirds diagonally
1 red bell pepper, cored and seeded
2 scallions, sliced diagonally
1 tbsp sesame seeds, toasted
Dressing

1/2 C. vegetable oil
1/4 C. apple cider vinegar
4 tbsp soy sauce
1 1/2 tbsp dark sesame oil
1/2 tbsp honey
1 garlic clove, minced
1/2 tsp peeled grated ginger
1/2 tbsp sesame seeds, toasted
1/4 C. creamy peanut butter
2 tsp kosher salt
1/2 tsp ground black pepper

Directions

1. Before you do anything, preheat the oven to 350 F.
2. Place a large pot of water over medium high heat. Bring it to a boil.
3. Stir in it the asparagus with a pinch of salt. Let it cook for 4 to 6 min or until it becomes tender.
4. Run the asparagus under some cold water. Drain it.
5. Coat the chicken breasts with oil. Season them with some salt and pepper.
6. Place them on a baking sheet. Place them in the oven and let them cook for 36 to 45 min
7. Slice the peppers and chicken breasts into stripes.
8. Get a small mixing bowl: Whisk in it the dressing ingredients.
9. Get a serving bowl: Toss in it the chicken with asparagus, sliced peppers, and dressing
10. Adjust the seasoning of the salad then serve it.
11. Enjoy.

Tarragon Zucchini

Prep Time: 2 mins
Total Time: 15 mins

Servings per Recipe: 6
Calories   149.3
Fat   10.6g
Cholesterol   18.1mg
Sodium   467.7mg
Carbohydrates   9.0g
Protein   5.2g

Ingredients
- 1/4 C. white vinegar
- 3/4 tsp salt
- 1/2 tsp pepper
- 1 tsp dried tarragon
- 1/2 C. mayonnaise
- 3 medium zucchini
- 3 oz. Swiss cheese, shredded

Directions
1. Place a small saucepan over medium heat. Stir in it the vinegar with tarragon, salt and pepper.
2. Cook them until they start boiling. Turn off the heat and let the mixture cool down.
3. Mix in the mayonnaise to make the sauce.
4. Before you do anything, preheat the grill and grease it.
5. Coat the zucchinis with some of the mayo sauce. Place them on the grill and let them cook for 6 min.
6. Flip the zucchini slices and lay over them some cheese. Let them cook for an extra 3 min.
7. Serve your grilled zucchinis warm.
8. Enjoy.

WASHINGTON
Country Turkey Roast

Prep Time: 2 days
Total Time: 52 h

Servings per Recipe: 10
Calories 1263.9
Fat 56.0g
Cholesterol 364.8mg
Sodium 14467.6mg
Carbohydrates 92.8g
Protein 95.6g

Ingredients
1 1/4 C. kosher salt
4 1/2 C. sugar
6 sprigs parsley
6 sprigs dill
6 sprigs thyme
6 sprigs tarragon
6 sprigs sage
2 sprigs rosemary
2 tsp mustard seeds
2 tsp fennel seeds
2 cinnamon sticks
5 bay leaves
8 whole cloves
1/2 tbsp juniper berries
1 tsp cardamom pod
2 tsp black peppercorns
2 lemons, sliced
2 gallons water
1 (14 lb.) whole turkey, rinsed
1 C. clarified butter

Directions
1. Get a bucket: Combine in it the spices with herbs, and lemon. Mix them well.
2. Heat the water until it starts boiling. Add it to the spice mix and stir them well to make the brine.
3. Place it aside and let the brine cool down completely.
4. Dip in it the turkey then let it sit for 2 days while turning it every once in a while.
5. Before you do anything, preheat the oven to 300 F.
6. Remove the turkey from the brine and dry it. Place it in a large roasting dish.
7. Rinse a thick cheesecloth then squeeze it dry. coat it with butter then coat the whole turkey with it.
8. Place the turkey in the oven and let it cook for 4 h. Baste it every once in a while with the remaining butter and juices from the pan.
9. Once the time is up, cover the turkey with a piece of foil. Let it rest for 40 min then serve it.
10. Enjoy.

Beacon Hill Brussels Sprouts

Prep Time: 15 mins
Total Time: 35 mins

Servings per Recipe: 6
Calories   247.8
Fat   14.5g
Cholesterol   14.9mg
Sodium   501.7mg
Carbohydrates   25.2g
Protein   7.4g

Ingredients
- 2 tbsp extra virgin olive oil
- 4 oz. thick-cut turkey bacon
- 1 1/2 lbs. Brussels sprouts, trimmed and halved through stem
- 3/4 tsp kosher salt
- 3/4 tsp ground black pepper
- 3/4 C. golden raisin
- 1 3/4 C. chicken stock

Directions
1. Place a pan over medium heat. Heat in it the oil. Cook in it the bacon until it becomes crisp.
2. Drain it and place it aside. Stir the Brussels sprouts with a pinch of salt and pepper into the pan.
3. Let them cook for 6 min while stirring it often. Stir in the stock with raisins.
4. Lower the heat and let them cook for 16 min over low heat.
5. Once the time is up, stir in the bacon. Serve your stir fry Brussels sprouts warm.
6. Enjoy.

SEATTLE
Compote

🥣 Prep Time: 10 mins
🕐 Total Time: 50 mins

Servings per Recipe: 6
Calories   208.5
Fat   0.3g
Cholesterol   0.0mg
Sodium   102.2mg
Carbohydrates   54.7g
Protein   1.4g

Ingredients
2 C. water
1/2 C. sugar
1/2 tsp ground cinnamon
1/4 tsp ground cloves
1/4 tsp salt
4 oz. dried apricots, chopped
4 oz. pitted dried plums, chopped
4 oz. dried pear halves, chopped

Directions
1. Place a heavy saucepan over medium heat. Combine in it the water, sugar, cinnamon, cloves and salt.
2. Stir in the fruits. Bring them to a gentle simmer. Put on the lid and lower the heat. Let them cook for 35 min.
3. Once the time is up, remove the lid. keep cooking the compote for an extract 12 min until it becomes thick.
4. Turn off the heat and let the compote cool down completely. Serve it with some ice cream.
5. Enjoy.

Baguette Lunch Box Salad

Prep Time: 25 mins
Total Time: 35 mins

Servings per Recipe: 6
Calories   387.9
Fat   22.2g
Cholesterol   29.8mg
Sodium   536.8mg
Carbohydrates   34.5g
Protein   14.1g

Ingredients

- 1 small baguette
- 1/3 C. extra virgin olive oil
- 1/3 C. lemon juice
- 2 tbsp diced shallots
- 2 tsp minced garlic
- 1 1/2 lbs. grape tomatoes, halved
- 8 oz. mozzarella cheese, cut into pieces
- 3 C. frisee
- kosher salt
- ground black pepper
- 1/4 C. roughly chopped basil

Directions

1. Before you do anything, preheat the grill and grease it.
2. Slice the baguette in half then cut each half into 4 pieces. Place the bread quarters on the grill.
3. Let them cook for 3 to 5 min on each side. Place them aside to cool down.
4. Slice the bread slices into 1/2 inch cubes.
5. Get a mixing bowl: Combine it the cubed bread with the remaining ingredients.
6. Place the salad in the fridge and let it sit for 25 to 35 min.
7. Garnish your salad with some basil then serve it.
8. Enjoy.

CHICKEN SOUP
Seattle

Prep Time: 10 mins
Total Time: 40 mins

Servings per Recipe: 6
Calories 398.4
Fat 10.4g
Cholesterol 15.4mg
Sodium 961.0mg
Carbohydrates 62.6g
Protein 16.1g

Ingredients
2 C. medium-grain brown rice, cooked
1 (28 oz.) cans diced tomatoes
6 C. low sodium chicken broth
2 large chicken breast halves, bone-in & skin-on
1 large yellow onion, small dice
2 tbsp canola oil
2 tsp dried oregano
2 tsp kosher salt
cayenne pepper

2 limes, juice
1 jalapeno, seeded and minced
Garish
avocado, diced
tortilla chips, crushed
lime wedge
Cotija cheese, crumbled
cilantro, chopped

Directions
1. Cut each chicken breast in half.
2. Place a large pot over medium heat. Heat in it 1 tbsp of oil. Cook in it 3/4 of the onion for 4 min.
3. Drain it and place it aside. Heat the remaining oil in the same pot.
4. Season the chicken pieces with some salt and pepper.
5. Place them in the hot oil and let them cook for 3 to 5 min on each side.
6. Stir in the cooked onion with tomato, broth and jalapeno. Let them cook until they start boiling over high heat.
7. Stir in the oregano with a pinch of salt. Let them cook for 22 min over low heat uncovered.
8. Once the time is up, drain the chicken and turn off the heat.
9. Allow the chicken pieces to cool down for a while. Shred it then stir it back into the soup pot.
10. Add to it the cayenne pepper with lime juice. Heat the soup for few minutes then serve warm.
11. Garnish it with some shredded cheese.
12. Enjoy.

Seattle Red Potato Salad

Prep Time: 30 mins
Total Time: 30 mins

Servings per Recipe: 6
Calories   256.4
Fat   13.4g
Cholesterol   16.8mg
Sodium   725.9mg
Carbohydrates   26.5g
Protein   7.9g

Ingredients
- 6 C. bite-sized cubed red potatoes
- 1 tsp salt
- 1 C. diced celery
- 1/2-1 C. chopped red onions
- 1/4 C. chopped parsley
- 1/4 C. red wine vinegar
- 3 tbsp extra virgin olive oil
- 1/2 tsp ground black pepper
- 1 C. crumbled blue cheese
- salt

Directions
1. Place a large saucepan of salted over high heat. Add to it the potato and cook them until they start boiling.
2. Lower the heat and let them cook until they become soft. Drain them.
3. Get a serving bowl: Stir in it the hot potatoes with celery, red onions, and parsley.
4. Add the vinegar, oil, and pepper. Toss them to coat.
5. Stir in the blue cheese then serve your salad right away. Or place it in the fridge for 25 min.
6. Enjoy.

SIMPLE
Cream of Meatball

🥣 Prep Time: 8 h 5 mins
🕐 Total Time: 9 h

Servings per Recipe: 20
Calories   427 kcal
Carbohydrates   8.8 g
Cholesterol   98 mg
Fat   35.4 g
Fiber   2.7 g
Protein   17.2 g
Sodium   962 mg

Ingredients
5 pounds Italian meatballs
1 (10.75 oz.) can condensed cream of mushroom soup
3/4 C. water
2 C. sour cream

Directions
1. Get a container and mix your sour cream, meatballs, water, and mushroom together. Place a lid on the container and place it in the fridge for 8 hrs.
2. Now add everything to your slow cooker and cook for about 3 to 4 hours on medium until the meat is completely cooked.

Leschi Park Avocado Shrimp Croissants

🥣 Prep Time: 15 mins
🕐 Total Time: 30 mins

Servings per Recipe: 4
Calories   777.3
Fat   48.1g
Cholesterol   333.6mg
Sodium   1271.8mg
Carbohydrates   51.4g
Protein   37.1g

Ingredients
- 2 eggs, hard boiled and diced
- 1 lb. large shrimp, shelled and deveined
- 1 avocado, diced
- 2/3 C. mayonnaise
- 2 tbsp chili sauce
- 2 tbsp green onions, chopped
- 2 tsp Worcestershire sauce
- 2 tsp red wine vinegar
- 1/4 tsp salt
- 1/8 tsp pepper
- 1/2 C. toasted sliced almonds
- 4 large croissants
- lettuce leaf

Directions
1. Place a 3 quarts saucepan over high heat. Fill 2 inches of it with water. Cook them until they start boiling.
2. Stir into it the shrimp and blanch it for 1 to 2 min until it becomes soft.
3. Drain the shrimp. Place the 4 shrimps with tail and place them aside for garnish.
4. Cut the remaining shrimp into dices.
5. Get a shallow serving bowl: Whisk in it the mayo with chili sauce, green onions, Worcestershire sauce, vinegar, salt and pepper.
6. Add the eggs with avocado, and shrimp. Toss them to coat. Stir in the almonds.
7. Cut each croissant in half. Lay a lettuce leaf on the bottom half.
8. Place in it some of the shrimp salad mix. Cover it with the top half.
9. Serve your shrimp croissants right away.
10. Enjoy.

LOX
Beau Monde
Sandwiches

🥣 Prep Time: 20 mins
🕐 Total Time: 30 mins

Servings per Recipe: 16
Calories   209.6
Fat   12.0g
Cholesterol   36.6mg
Sodium   722.6mg
Carbohydrates   16.5g
Protein   8.8g

Ingredients
1 lb. loaf rye bread
3/4 lb. lox, sliced (brined salmon)
16 oz. cream cheese, softened
1/4 C. milk
2 tbsp dill, chopped
2 tbsp squeezed lemon juice
1/2-1 tsp beau monde seasoning

10 chives, chopped
red onion, sliced
capers

Directions
1. Before you do anything, preheat the oven to 350 F.
2. Slice the off the crust of the bread slices. Slice each bread slice into 4 pieces.
3. Lay the bread slices on two lined baking trays. Place them in the oven and let them cook for 11 min.
4. Once the time is up, place them aside to cool down.
5. Get a mixing bowl: Beat in it the cream cheese until it becomes smooth. Mix in the milk and whip them until they become soft.
6. Mix in the spices with dill and lemon juice. Spoon 2 tbsp of the mix into each bread sliced.
7. Garnish them with some chives and onion slices. Serve them right away.
8. Enjoy.

Butterscotch Squares from Seattle

🥣 Prep Time: 35 mins
🕐 Total Time: 1 h

Servings per Recipe: 24
Calories   158.6
Fat   9.4g
Cholesterol   22.8mg
Sodium   140.3mg
Carbohydrates   16.6g
Protein   2.6g

Ingredients

1 1/2 C. raw unsalted cashews
1 tsp salt, divided
1/2 C. butter
1/2 C. brown sugar, packed
1 egg
2 tsp pure vanilla extract

1 3/4 C. unbleached white flour
Syrup
3 tbsp butter
1/3 C. sugar
2 tbsp water

Directions

1. To make the cookie pan:
2. Before you do anything, preheat the oven to 350 F. Grease a baking pan and place it aside.
3. Grease a baking sheet with butter then dust them with some flour.
4. Spread the cashews on a baking sheet. Cook them in the oven for 8 min.
5. Allow the almonds to cool down completely. Toss them with 3/4 tsp of salt. Let them cool down.
6. Place a saucepan over medium heat. Heat in it the butter until it melts and become golden brown.
7. Strain the melted butter and place it aside to cool down for 11 min in the fridge.
8. Get a mixing bowl: Mix in it the butter with brown sugar, egg and vanilla until they become smooth and creamy.
9. Add 1/4 tsp of salt with half of the flour. Mix them well.
10. Mix in the remaining flour until you get a smooth dough. Transfer the dough to the greased and floured sheet.
11. Press it with your hands until it covers it. Place it aside.
12. To make the syrup:
13. Place a heavy saucepan over medium heat. Stir in the sugar with butter until it they start bubbling.
14. Mix in the water and stir them well until they melt. Stir in the cashews.
15. Pour the syrup all over the dough layer. Place it in the oven and let it cook for 26 min.
16. Allow the cookie pan to cool down completely. Slice it into bars then serve them.
17. Enjoy.

SWEET
Ginger Cookies

Prep Time: 20 mins
Total Time: 31 mins

Servings per Recipe: 36
Calories 149.1
Fat 5.8g
Cholesterol 18.5mg
Sodium 135.3mg
Carbohydrates 22.6g
Protein 1.8g

Ingredients
1/2 C. butter, softened
1/2 C. shortening
1 1/2 C. sugar
1/2 C. molasses
2 eggs, beaten
4 C. flour
1/2 tsp salt

2 1/4 tsp baking soda
2 1/2 tsp ginger
1 1/2 tsp cloves
1 1/2 tsp cinnamon

Directions
1. Before you do anything, preheat the oven to 350 F.
2. Get a mixing bowl: Beat in it the butter, shortening and sugar until they become smooth and light.
3. Add the eggs with molasses. Mix them well.
4. Get a mixing bowl: Stir in it the flour with salt, baking soda, ginger, cloves and cinnamon.
5. Add the flour mixture to the cream mix. Combine them well until you get a soft dough.
6. Shape the dough into 1 inch balls. Roll them in sugar then place them on a baking sheet
7. Place the cookies sheet in the oven. Cook them for 11 to 12 min.
8. Allow the cookies to cool down completely then serve them.
9. Enjoy.

Tomatoes Stuffed

Prep Time: 15 mins
Total Time: 23 mins

Servings per Recipe: 6
Calories   174.7
Fat   12.6g
Cholesterol   26.5mg
Sodium   224.8mg
Carbohydrates   7.5g
Protein   9.3g

Ingredients
- 6 tomatoes
- 1/4 lb. shredded turkey bacon
- 1 garlic clove, chopped
- 1/2 C. sage, chopped
- 1 tbsp extra virgin olive oil
- 6 oz. goat cheese
- 1 - 2 oz. parmesan cheese

Directions
1. Before you do anything, preheat the oven broiler.
2. Slice off the tops of the tomatoes. Use a spoon the hollow them.
3. Place a small skillet over medium heat. Heat in it the oil. Cook in it the garlic for 40 sec.
4. Stir in the sage with 3/4 of the turkey bacon. Cook them for 2 min.
5. Transfer the mixture to a blender. Add to them the goat cheese. Pulse them several times to mix them and make the filling.
6. Spoon the filling into the hollow tomatoes. Sprinkle the parmesan cheese on top.
7. Place the tomatoes in a baking dish. Cook them in the oven for 4 to 6 min until they cheese melts.
8. Garnish your stuffed tomato with the remaining bacon. Serve them warm.
9. Enjoy.

MEDITERRANEAN
Seasoned Chicken with Yogurt Salsa

Prep Time: 15 mins
Total Time: 25 mins

Servings per Recipe: 2
Calories   518.4
Fat   8.5g
Cholesterol   136.5mg
Sodium   2090.0mg
Carbohydrates   41.0g
Protein   69.7g

Ingredients

2 C. plain fat-free yogurt, divided
3 medium garlic cloves, minced, divided
2 tbsp rosemary leaves, chopped
1 tsp lemon zest
4 tbsp lemon juice
1 tsp sea salt
1 lb. uncooked boneless skinless chicken breast, cut into pieces
cooking spray
2 large sweet red peppers, cut into pieces

1 large cucumber, seeded and cut into pieces
1/4 C. red onion, chopped
1 tbsp parsley, chopped
2 tsp olive oil
1/2 tsp table salt
1/4 tsp ground black pepper

Directions

1. Before you do anything, preheat the grill and grease it.
2. Get a mixing bowl: Whisk in it 1 1/2 C. yogurt, 2 chopped garlic cloves, rosemary and lemon juice.
3. Stir in the chicken pieces and toss them to coat. Let them sit for 30 min to 8 h.
4. Thread the pepper dices and chicken pieces into skewers. Grill them for 4 to 6 min on each side until they are done.
5. Get a mixing bowl: Stir in it the cucumber, onion, remaining 1/2 C. of yogurt, remaining chopped garlic clove, parsley, oil, salt and pepper to make the salsa.
6. Serve your chicken skewers warm with the yogurt salsa.
7. Enjoy.

Enchiladas Washington Style

🥣 Prep Time: 10 mins
🕐 Total Time: 55 mins

Servings per Recipe: 6
Calories   541.8
Fat   41.1g
Cholesterol   82.9mg
Sodium   1263.4mg
Carbohydrates   28.7g
Protein   16.4g

Ingredients

12 crisp taco shells
8 oz. cheddar cheese, grated
2 (10 3/4 oz.) cans condensed cream of chicken soup
16 oz. sour cream
1 (4 oz.) cans diced green chilies
2 C. leftover chicken, diced
milk

Directions

1. Before you do anything, preheat the oven to 375 F. Coat a casserole dish with a cooking spray.
2. Get a mixing bowl: Mix in it the sour cream with the chicken soup. Stir in the chicken with chilies.
3. Place the taco shells in the greased casserole. Spoon the chicken mixture into the shells to fill them.
4. Sprinkle the cheese on top. Pour the remaining chicken mixture on top.
5. Place the casserole in the oven and let it cook for 46 min. Serve it hot.
6. Enjoy.

ISAMELLE'S
Enchiladas

Prep Time: 20 mins
Total Time: 45 mins

Servings per Recipe: 6
Calories 525.1
Fat 31.6g
Cholesterol 116.8mg
Sodium 1023.4mg
Carbohydrates 26.5g
Protein 33.9g

Ingredients
1 (10 oz.) cans enchilada sauce
1 (15 oz.) cans tomato sauce
2 tsp chili powder
12 small corn tortillas
1 1/2 lbs. ground beef
1 small yellow onion, small diced
8 oz. medium cheddar, grated
salt & pepper
cayenne pepper

vegetable oil
Topping
sour cream
diced avocado
chopped cilantro
salsa
chopped tomato
sliced black olives

Directions
1. Before you do anything, preheat the oven to 325 F. Grease a casserole dish.
2. Place a saucepan over medium heat. Stir in it the tomato sauce with chili powder. Heat in it the sauce for few minutes.
3. Place a pan over medium heat. Cook in it the ground beef over high heat for 4 min. Drain half of the excess fat from the pan.
4. Add the onion with a pinch of salt and pepper. Cook them for 6 min to make the filling.
5. Place a large frying pan over medium heat. Heat about in it about 1/4 inch of vegetable oil.
6. Lay in it a tortilla. Cook it for 35 sec. Drain it and place on a paper towel. Cover it with another paper towel.
7. Repeat the process with the remaining tortillas. Spread a thin layer of tomato sauce in the bottom of the casserole dish.
8. Place 3 tbsp of the filling on each tortilla. Top them with some cheese then roll them.
9. Place them in the casserole on top of the sauce layer with the seam facing down.
10. Drizzle the rest of the sauce on top of the tortillas following by the cheese.
11. Place the casserole in the oven. Let it cook for 6 min.
12. Serve your tortillas casserole warm.
13. Enjoy.

Whipped Chocolate Pie

🥣 Prep Time: 15 mins
🕐 Total Time: 50 mins

Servings per Recipe: 8
Calories   641.2
Fat   54.5g
Cholesterol   147.9mg
Sodium   193.6mg
Carbohydrates   40.5g
Protein   10.6g

Ingredients

1 unbaked pie shell, 9-inch diameter with high-fluted crust
2 C. milk, divided
1 3/4 C. heavy whipping cream, divided
1/2 C. sugar
2 large eggs
3 tbsp cornstarch
10 oz. semisweet chocolate, chopped
1/4 C. unsalted butter
1 1/2 tsp pure vanilla extract, divided

Directions

1. Before you do anything, preheat the oven to 340 F. Position the rack on the away from the heat source.
2. Pierce the pie shell several times with a fork. Lay a piece of foil over it to cover it
3. Pour over it some dry beans.
4. Place the pie shell in the oven and let it cook for 13 min.
5. Once the time is up, discard the beans and foil sheet. Bake the shell for an extra 10 min.
6. Place it aside to cool down for a while.
7. Place a heavy saucepan over medium heat. Stir in it 1 1/2 C. milk and 1 C. cream and heat them until they become hot.
8. Get a mixing bowl: Mix in it the remaining milk with sugar, eggs and cornstarch until no lumps are found.
9. Ladle some of the hot cream mixture into the cold milk mix. Mix them well. Stir the mixture into the hot cream in the saucepan.
10. Heat them until they start boiling while whisking them at the same time.
11. Turn off the heat and stir in the chocolate with butter and 1 tsp of vanilla until they melt and become smooth.
12. Use a mesh sieve to strain the batter. Lay over it a parchment sheet to cover it. Chill it in the fridge until it cools down.
13. Pour the chocolate filling after it cools down into the cool pie shell. Place it in the fridge and let chill for at least 2 h 30 min.
14. Get a mixing bowl: Beat in it the vanilla extract with the rest of the cream until their soft peaks.
15. Pie the whipped cream on top of the tart. Serve it with your favorite toppings.
16. Enjoy.

MADRONA
Chocolate Puffs

🥣 Prep Time: 10 mins
🕐 Total Time: 50 mins

Servings per Recipe: 12
Calories 369.5
Fat 27.1g
Cholesterol 150.5mg
Sodium 226.5mg
Carbohydrates 28.2g
Protein 5.0g

Ingredients
Pastry
1 C. water
1/2 C. butter
1 C. all-purpose flour
4 eggs
Filling
1 (3 1/2 oz.) vanilla instant pudding mix
1 C. milk

2 C. heavy whipping cream, well chilled
Glaze
1 oz. unsweetened chocolate
1 tbsp butter
1 C. confectioners' sugar
2 tbsp hot water

Directions
1. To make the puffs:
2. Before you do anything, preheat the oven to 400 F.
3. Get a mixing bowl:
4. Place a saucepan over medium heat. Combine in it the water with butter. Heat them through until they start boiling.
5. Add the flour and combine them until no lumps are found. Keep stirring them until the batter from a ball.
6. Turn off the heat and transfer the mixture to a large mixing bowl.
7. Add the eggs gradually while mixing all the time until they become smooth.
8. Drop 1/4 C. mounds of the mix into a lined up baking sheet. Place it in the oven and let them cook for 36 to 42 min.
9. Once the time is up, place the puffs aside to cool down completely.
10. To make the filling:
11. Get a mixing bowl: Beat in it the milk with pudding well. Mix in the whipping cream for 2 min until its peak starts forming.
12. Place the filling in the fridge and let it sit until ready to use.
13. To make the icing:
14. Place a heavy saucepan over medium heat. Stir in it the butter with chocolate. Stir them until they melt.
15. Turn off the heat and mix in the confectioner sugar with 2 tbsp of hot water.
16. Slice off the tops of the puffs. Spoon the filling into them.
17. Cover them with their sliced top then drizzle the icing on top.
18. Serve your stuffed puffs with some tea.
19. Enjoy.

Spicy Tofu Pesto

Prep Time: 20 mins
Total Time: 20 mins

Servings per Recipe: 8
Calories	91.6
Fat	8.2g
Cholesterol	0.0mg
Sodium	148.2mg
Carbohydrates	3.0g
Protein	2.7g

Ingredients

- 1/2 C. toasted whole almond
- 1 1/2 C. loosely packed cilantro leaves
- 1 large garlic clove, minced
- 1/2 C. crumbled firm tofu
- 3 tbsp lime juice
- 2 tbsp olive oil
- 1/2 tsp salt
- 1 small green chile, chopped, seeded

Directions

1. Get a blender: Place in it the almonds. Pulse them several times until they become chopped.
2. Mix in the remaining ingredients. Blend them smooth.
3. Spoon the pesto into an airtight jar. Serve it right away or place it in the fridge for 2 to 3 days.
4. Enjoy.

LAKE WASHINGTON
Cookies

🍳 Prep Time: 30 mins
🕐 Total Time: 1 h 30 mins

Servings per Recipe: 60
Calories 99.3
Fat 3.7g
Cholesterol 10.5mg
Sodium 50.5mg
Carbohydrates 15.5g
Protein 1.2g

Ingredients
Cookie
- 1 1/2 C. raisins
- 1 C. water
- 1 C. shortening
- 1 1/2 C. sugar
- 3 eggs, beaten
- 1 tsp vanilla extract
- 3 3/4 C. all-purpose flour
- 1 tsp baking powder
- 1 tsp baking soda
- 1/2 tsp salt

Topping
- 1/2 C. sugar
- 1 tsp cinnamon
- 1/2 tsp nutmeg

Directions
1. Before you do anything, preheat the oven to 375 F.
2. Place a heavy saucepan over medium heat. Stir in it the water with raisins. Cook them until they start boiling.
3. Lower the heat and let them cook until the raisins absorbs all the water.
4. Get a mixing bowl: Mix in it the dry ingredients.
5. Get a mixing bowl: Beat in it the shortening with sugar until they become smooth. Mix in the eggs with vanilla and cream.
6. Add the dry ingredients mix gradually while mixing all the time until you get a soft dough.
7. Fold the raisins mix into the dough.
8. Get a small shallow bowl: Stir in the nutmeg with sugar and cinnamon.
9. Shape the dough into bite size balls. Coat them with the sugar mix. Place them on a cookie sheet.
10. Place the cookie sheet in the oven then let them cook for 10 to 11 min.
11. Allow the cookies to cool down completely then serve them.
12. Enjoy.

Perfect Seattle Chili

Prep Time: 30 mins
Total Time: 2 h 50 mins

Servings per Recipe: 8
Calories	311 kcal
Fat	12.8 g
Carbohydrates	32.2g
Protein	19.7 g
Cholesterol	32 mg
Sodium	641 mg

Ingredients
- 3 tbsps vegetable oil
- 1 green bell pepper, seeded and chopped
- 1 large onion, chopped
- 4 garlic cloves, minced
- 1/2 lb beef stew meat, cubed into 1-inch size
- 1/2 lb lean ground beef
- 1/2 lb dry red kidney beans, rinsed
- 1 (28-oz.) can crushed tomatoes with liquid
- 1 (14-oz.) can beef broth
- 1 tsp Italian seasoning
- 2 1/2 tbsps red chili powder
- 2 tbsps brown sugar
- Salt, to taste

Directions
1. In a large pan, heat the oil with medium heat.
2. Add the bell pepper and onion and sauté for about 3-4 minutes.
3. Add the garlic and sauté for about 1 minute.
4. Add the stew meat and ground beef and cook for about 8-10 minutes or till browned.
5. Stir in the beans, tomatoes and broth.
6. Cover and bring to a boil.
7. Let everything boil for about 4-5 minutes.
8. Uncover and stir in the remaining ingredients and reduce the heat to low.
9. Simmer, uncovered for about 2 hours or till desired doneness.

JALAPENO
Maple Chili

🥣 Prep Time: 25 mins
🕐 Total Time: 1 h 45 mins

Servings per Recipe: 8
Calories	741 kcal
Fat	32.2 g
Carbohydrates	59.2g
Protein	49.3 g
Cholesterol	142 mg
Sodium	865 mg

Ingredients
2 tbsps olive oil
1 red bell pepper, seeded and chopped
1 large onion, chopped
2 garlic cloves, mince
2 jalapeno peppers, seeded and chopped
1 (40-oz.) can kidney beans, rinsed and drained
1 (28-oz.) can crushed tomatoes with liquid
1 (15-oz.) can tomato sauce
3/4 C. maple syrup
2 tbsps red chili powder
Freshly ground black pepper, to taste
4 lbs ground beef chuck
Salt, to taste

Directions
1. In a large pan, heat oil with medium heat.
2. Add the bell pepper and onion and sauté for about 5-6 minutes.
3. Add the garlic and jalapeno and sauté for about 1 minute.
4. Add the beans, tomatoes, tomato sauce, maple syrup, red chili and black pepper and bring to a boil.
5. Reduce the heat to low.
6. Meanwhile heat a large nonstick skillet on medium-high heat.
7. Add the beef and sprinkle with salt.
8. Cook everything for about 8-10 minutes.
9. Discard the excess fat and transfer the beef into a pan with the beans mixture.
10. Simmer, stirring occasionally for about 1 hour.
11. Then add in the salt.

Made in the USA
Las Vegas, NV
15 July 2021